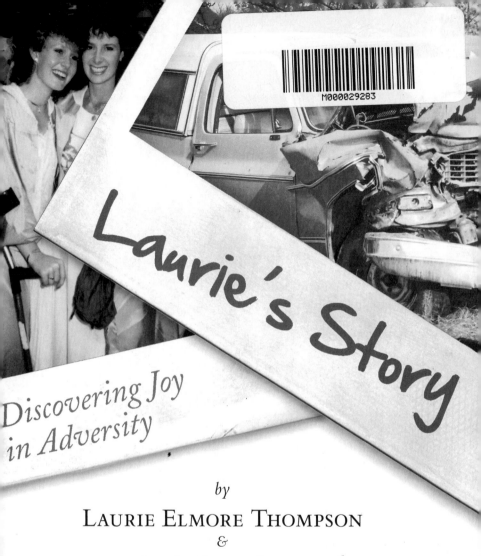

Laurie's Story

Discovering Joy in Adversity

by

LAURIE ELMORE THOMPSON

&

LAURA HODGES POOLE

AMBASSADOR INTERNATIONAL

GREENVILLE, SOUTH CAROLINA & BELFAST, NORTHERN IRELAND

www.ambassador-international.com

Laurie's Story
Discovering Joy in Adversity

© 2011 by Laurie Elmore Thompson

Printed in the United States of America

ISBN: 9781935507772

Cover Design by David Siglin of A&E Media
Page Layout by Kelley Moore of Points & Picas

AMBASSADOR INTERNATIONAL
Emerald House
427 Wade Hampton Blvd.
Greenville, SC 29609, USA
www.ambassador-international.com

AMBASSADOR BOOKS
The Mount
2 Woodstock Link
Belfast, BT6 8DD, Northern Ireland, UK
www.ambassador-international.com

The colophon is a trademark of Ambassador

Dedication

I, first and foremost, dedicate this book to my Lord and Savior, Jesus Christ. Without Him, I would have no story.

To my family, this book is in honor of all we have overcome together.

To Dad, thank you for remembering horrific details so I could be accurate in my representation here.

To Kevin, you are such a gift from God. Thank you for being my helpmate, lover and best friend.

To Luke, Lydiaruth and Canaan, I praise God for allowing me to be your mother. May this book inspire you to know your Savior more deeply, so that He permeates every aspect of your lives for eternity.

Laurie has chosen to use her unique, challenging life experiences to write an honest perspective that speaks to the faithfulness of God no matter what our circumstances. Individuals, with and without a disability, will be encouraged and challenged to see our response to adversity as a choice.... to draw closer to the One who loves us unconditionally and as a result, be used by God! Laurie has made that choice and it is powerfully reflective in her speaking, singing and life.

—Christine Hillesheim, Director, Joni and Friends Charlotte

Laurie's Story: Discovering Joy in Adversity powerfully communicates the story of a young woman's struggle to overcome a tragic accident which left her paralyzed from the waist down. The vulnerability with which she shares her journey will cause the reader's heart to ache with empathy. Yet, her focus on the grace of God draws one's eyes heavenward to gaze upon the All Sufficient One.

—Bill Jones, D. Min.
President, Columbia International University

Someone has wisely said, 'The mark of the mature Christian is not what happens to them, but how they respond to what happens to them!" In this wonderful book, Laurie Thompson clearly shows that she has that special touch of maturity. Her response to a tragic accident is an incredible testimony to her love for Jesus and her determination to be "above her problems" rather than beneath them. All who read this book will be greatly blessed by this remarkable and gifted Christian.

—Evangelist Junior Hill

Foreword

TEACHING A CLASS AT THE American Christian Writers Workshop in Anderson, South Carolina, I couldn't take my eyes off a striking young woman who soon became a dear friend— and one of the most fascinating Christian women I've ever met. She was young and beautiful, with the most gorgeous green eyes and strawberry-blond hair I had ever seen. Oh, yes, and one other remarkable characteristic I noticed as she stood to leave the class: she walked by slinging her feet ahead of her, one at the time, supported by one cane, as she walked vigorously out of the room.

Laurie was a leader among the other writers, driving them to the restaurant for lunch, encouraging first one, then another. She chatted cheerfully, yet spent tender times with each new friend, learning about them, asking about their lives and their families. Her laugh was contagious. I felt privileged to meet this exceptionally talented Christian, who lived life to the fullest. Since that writers' workshop, I have grown to respect Laurie even more as a sister in Christ, a humble Christian wife and mother, and one of the most capable Christians I know.

This book flows easily, portraying a realistic version of Laurie's life story. You'll find her special personality on its pages. She'll take you through the initial journey of her family as a drunken driver crossed the median on a large highway one night and destroyed their pickup truck with two sleeping girls in the back under the camper top. You will go along with her to a hospital where a drunken doctor left her bleeding, lying on a gurney for hours in a broom closet, and removed the neck brace from her younger sister, who had spine damage. When he was about to perform surgery on her mother in a hallway, Laurie's loving father, with the help of a sheriff, had the courage to move his family to another hospital.

In spite of the tragedy, Laurie's life has been filled with grace and dignity. She has learned to walk, ride horseback, swim, graduate from college and seminaries, work to put her husband through school, give birth to three children, and engage in a vibrant singing and speaking ministry.

The closing chapters of the book will inspire you as Laurie shares her understanding of God's truth about suffering and adversity. She defines the "Adversity Effect," giving a clear explanation of God's will for our lives and the value of adversity in any Christian's life. Her words of wisdom will encourage teens and adults alike. I am honored to write the foreword to this worthy book.

—EDNA M. ELLISON, Ph.D.
Speaker, Humorist and Christian Mentoring Guru
www.ednaellison.com

Contents

Chapter One

The Accident

THE FALL QUARTER OF SCHOOL was drawing to a close, and the Thanksgiving holiday was rapidly approaching. My parents, Wayne and Sue Elmore, were busy with preparations for the holiday. My nine-year-old sister, Kim, and I were ecstatic to be getting out of school for several days and heading to Florida for Thanksgiving break. I was fourteen years old at the time.

My family was looking forward to spending the holiday in Clermont, Florida, where we traditionally vacationed twice a year. We would be staying with my Uncle Ty, Mom's youngest brother. Kim and I could hardly contain our excitement.

Me with Mom, Kim and Uncle Ty in his citrus grove in Clermont, Florida

Our previous visits to Uncle Ty's house had been so much fun. Kim and I thought his bachelor pad was pretty cool. A lake right across from his front porch provided activities such as swimming, fishing, and boating. The lake was always so warm. I savored the feeling of the sand oozing between my toes and the water rising around my ankles and up my legs as I waded into the water. It was all I could think about during those cold November days in South Carolina before we left.

Uncle Ty owned a nursery and landscaping business. His shop was entertaining because Kim and I helped customers and pretended we were running the business. We thought we were pretty big stuff.

Because we were going to travel through the night, Dad fixed up the camper part of our silver Chevrolet pickup with a large piece of carpet, a dome light, a beanbag chair, a portable television set, two folding chairs, and our walkie-talkies. Kim and I packed several items to keep us occupied on the trip. We took various toys, games, cards, and, most importantly, snacks.

Finally, the day arrived. It was the day before Thanksgiving, Wednesday, November 24, 1982. As soon as school let out that afternoon, we were anxious to get on the road. After making sure the dogs were taken care of and locking the house, there was only one thing left to do before driving off. As we sat on the tailgate of the truck, Mom prayed as she usually did prior to our leaving on a trip. She simply prayed for safety in travel and gave thanks for our family.

We all took the prayer time very seriously, but with Mom's "amen" barely out of her mouth, Kim and I scrambled into the back of the truck. Smiling, Mom joined Dad in the cab of the truck. The plan was to travel through the night and arrive in Clermont early the next morning. Dad's rationale was that since there weren't usually many drivers on the road late at night, it would be the safest time to travel.

Kim and I were having a lot of fun as we played games and talked "girl talk." It wasn't long before we grew tired after having spent all day in school. Shortly after dark, we were fast asleep.

Dad pulled into Atlanta for a bathroom break, and we got ice cream cones while he filled the truck with gas. This far into the trip, it was all still an adventure. Having had a quick nap, Kim and I enjoyed the ice cream while we talked. But once the ice cream was finished, we quickly fell asleep. Shortly thereafter, Dad stopped again right outside of Atlanta.

Me with Mom, Kim, Uncle Ty and Uncle Travis at the Matlack Foliage Mart store

We stopped at a friend's Christmas tree farm to pick up a trailer-load of Christmas trees that Uncle Ty planned to sell at his shop, Matlack's Foliage Mart. Neither of us girls were pleased at being roused from our sleep a second time and having to sit in the cab while the adults hitched up the trailer. It was cold, and we were ready to be in Florida. The warm sand oozing around my toes was quickly becoming unimaginable. After what seemed like forever to us, we were finally on our way again.

In the early hours of Thanksgiving morning, Thursday, November 25, 1982, we were traveling on a four-lane highway, I-75 south, through the southern part of Georgia. It was approximately 12:30 a.m. when my dad noticed headlights swerving in the I-75 northbound lanes. The vehicle proceeded to come across the grassy median onto our side of the highway, hundreds of yards in front of our truck.

Just as quickly, the headlights disappeared, and Dad thought it must have been a highway patrolman turning around to go after someone. He dismissed any concerns until seconds later when the headlights returned from the right shoulder of the interstate. They seemed to bounce out of the grass right toward the road. The vehicle was now going north in our southbound lane!

Dad yelled to Mom, "My gosh, Sue, look at this!"

But Mom, being in a sound sleep, did not wake up. Dad began to slow down and turned hard right into the emergency lane. Horrifyingly, the other driver mirrored Dad's maneuver. Dad made another sharp turn toward the median to try to avoid a collision, to no avail. The other driver again matched that turn. Dad turned hard right and then turned left yet again in a desperate attempt to get out of the other driver's way. But it was too late. We were hit head-on by the driver traveling at over fifty-five mph.

I awoke to the horrific sound of brakes screeching. I lifted my head, trying hard to identify where I was. There were faint lights shining through the plastic window. Drowsily, I thought I must be having a weird dream. I laid my head back down to sleep. Accustomed to having terrible nightmares, I didn't realize that what I was hearing was really happening.

As the truck skidded and turned, there was an incredible amount of force pushing my body forward, totally out of my control. In the next instant, total chaos ensued as metal crashed and our bodies went flying amidst an eerie blackness. And then there was total silence.

Dad was in shock. The other driver lay in the road, hoarsely gasping for air. Dad's first impulse was to get out of the truck and beat him with a two-by-four that was lying among the debris from the wreck. But then he thought, "That poor guy didn't want to be in this accident any more than we did."

We later learned that when the other driver's truck door was opened at the tow yard, several liquor bottles fell out onto the ground. The other driver had been drunk. To amplify our frustrations, any hopes of filing charges against the uninsured, drunk driver were lost due to the fact that the sheriff's department misplaced his blood sample in the midst of the chaos.

In a state of shock, Dad sat unable to move in the truck. It took several minutes before he could even open his door. Finally, he opened it and fell to the ground beside the truck. Still unable to move the rest of his body, Dad lay perilously close to a line on the pavement. Sporadically, he felt strong gusts of wind against his head and was startled by the sudden bursts of noise. He then realized his head was right beside the middle line on the road and those gusts of wind were passing vehicles!

"Here I survived Vietnam and this car wreck, but now I'm going to get run over because I cannot move!" his mind screamed.

After what seemed an eternity to him, Dad was able to get up. He did not see Mom in the cab, so he assumed she had been thrown from the vehicle upon impact. Immediately, his thoughts turned to Kim and me in the back.

Our truck had been hit with such force that the engine had been pushed partially into the floorboard of the cab. Dazed, Dad saw that the Christmas trees had been thrown in disarray over the top of the camper and over the now-mangled hood, and the heat from the engine could ignite them—they were beginning to smolder. He knew he had to get us out before the truck was completely engulfed in flames.

Dad began beating on the plastic windows with the force of a madman. His hands were throbbing in pain and bleeding from the force of his blows. I awoke to Dad's agonizing screams.

"Laurie!!! Kim!!! Can you hear me?"

I knew something must be terribly wrong because of the tone of his voice. I lifted my head in the darkness and tried to respond. But where was I? *Why can't Daddy see me?* I remember thinking. I wanted to tell him where I was. *He sounds so upset…I'm right here.* My mouth opened, but no words would come. My throat felt tight, and I strained harder in an attempt to yell. Still nothing. It was as if I were in the middle of a nightmare, unable to cry for help. Then I lost consciousness again.

By this time, a county sheriff had stopped and called for emergency vehicles. Kim groped in the darkness for my body. She felt my legs and tried with all her might to pull me toward the end of the truck, but she simply didn't have the strength. Bystanders helped get Kim and me from the back of the pickup. Kim was removed first and instructed to lie still to prevent further damage to her injured body.

The paramedics asked Kim questions in an attempt to discern whether she had suffered any brain damage. But she was having a difficult time remaining conscious. Dad tried to keep her awake while at the same time keep an eye on me and try to figure out what had happened to Mom.

"Where is Sue? Where's my wife?" Dad yelled at the paramedics and the others who were on the scene.

No one had seen my mother.

"She was in the cab with me!" he screamed.

Leaving Kim's side, Dad ran back to double-check the cab. To his horror, he saw Mom crumpled under the smashed-in dashboard, unconscious. She was quickly removed from the smoldering truck. Kim and I had been placed on stretchers by the side of the highway. At this point, I awoke again. My left arm dangled limply over the side of the stretcher, and I felt the cool, damp grass on my fingertips. Dad knelt beside me. I saw desperation in his eyes as I peered into his face.

"Laurie, are you all right? Are you okay?" He asked repeatedly. His concern, anger, and fear over the situation were apparent.

Our truck after the accident

"I'm fine…where are Mommy and Kim?" I managed to reply.

His voice was reassuring me, telling me not to worry, but I was losing consciousness again. *Why does Daddy look so upset…I am so sleepy…*I still had no idea that we had been involved in a horrific head-on collision and that my life was slowly draining from me.

Dad's reassuring voice changed to fear as he realized I was slipping away. Upset, he yelled over and over for me to stay awake. His voice ebbed in and out of my mind, pulling me back time and time again. But I had lost a lot of blood. I could not stay awake for more than a few seconds at the time.

Although Dad's hands were badly injured, his pain wasn't registering in his mind. The only thing he knew for sure was that his wife and two daughters were dying before his eyes. Stuck in a remote rural location, emergency response was sorely lacking. Dad feared losing us all.

An assessment of our injuries was staggering. In the impact of the accident, a rifle that Dad kept on the gun-rack in the cab broke over the back of his neck. Mom suffered from a traumatic blow to the back of her head as well, and it was feared that she had some internal damage. Kim's little body was thrown with such force into the back of the cab that her neck had been broken near the base of her skull. I had been thrown up into the camper top, which crushed my back, and then I was thrown forward so that the left side of my face smashed through the portable television set. When I was removed from the vehicle, my left eye was literally hanging out of its socket.

Because of the holiday and the magnitude of the accident, several EMS workers and ambulances had to be recruited to the scene.

Another picture of our wrecked truck with part of the trailer with the Christmas trees seen on the left.

We were all taken to the nearest hospital. Incredibly, the first ambulance Mom and I were placed in ran out of gas—both tanks. We were transferred to one that had recently been in a repair shop. The engine was not working properly, so we had to be transferred to yet another ambulance before arriving at the hospital.

The hospital was actually a small medical clinic. It did not have the appropriate facilities to handle the severity of our injuries or the number of victims involved, but the personnel agreed to stabilize us. We had no way of knowing that the nightmare was just beginning.

God, in His mercy, had spared Dad of serious injury. Mom, Kim, and I would need someone to physically fight for our lives in the hours to come. Although shaken by the accident, Dad was that advocate. His presence proved to be life-saving...literally.

For some unknown reason, upon arrival, hospital personnel left Mom on a gurney in the hallway, where she lay curled up in a fetal position awaiting treatment. When Dad and Kim arrived, Kim was taken for X-rays. The ER doctor had me placed in a makeshift storage room similar to a closet.

I finally awoke while in that room, alone in complete silence. Dazed, I looked at my surroundings. The walls were solid white, and there was a broom or mop in the right corner. All I could think was, *Where am I? What is happening?* Everything was blurry. *Maybe I am dead.* Then it dawned on me—*I must be in heaven!* But then I quickly reasoned I couldn't be in heaven because my head resonated with pain, and I remembered reading in the Bible that there is no pain or suffering in heaven. *Surely I was not in the <u>other</u> place...*

My thoughts raced wildly as I slowly lifted my left hand to feel my face. My arm was so heavy and hard to control. I wasn't even sure my head was connected to my body! I discovered it was, of course, and this gave me a strange sense of relief. I lethargically brought my hand back down and was horrified to see it absolutely saturated with my own blood. I had never seen so much blood! It was dripping off my arm to the extent that I could not even see the color of my skin. As I began to lose consciousness, I realized I was bleeding to death.

While I was in that "storage room," Dad was with the doctor examining Kim in the X-ray room. A county sheriff was in the room watching what was going on. Dad wasn't sure of his motives and in his own confused state of mind thought angrily to himself, *"Doesn't this guy have anything better to do than to get his kicks by watching my family suffer?"*

Kim was wearing a neck collar that the paramedics had placed on her, but the doctor proceeded to take it off and began maneuvering her neck from side to side under the X-ray equipment. Impatiently, the doctor commanded Kim to lie still and cooperate. He aggressively continued to examine her as he barked commands.

Dad thought the doctor's behavior was incredibly strange and spoke up. "Can't you X-ray through the neck brace?"

The doctor very belligerently replied, "Who's the doctor here?"

Dad hesitated briefly, yet asked him again, "Is that the normal procedure for a broken neck?"

The doctor did not change his attitude or his approach. Dad knew that he was probably still in shock, so he tried to give the doctor the benefit of the doubt. After all, he *was* the doctor, Dad said to himself.

Shortly thereafter, the doctor decided to examine Mom where she had been left lying unconscious in the hallway. Once again, Dad was present while the examination took place. The doctor unfastened Mom's clothes. He felt and thumped on her stomach and then stated she had internal bleeding. Frantically, the doctor declared that she needed immediate surgery to save her life. He proceeded to pull out a scalpel as if he were going to operate right there!

At this point, Dad decided he had had enough. "What are you doing?" he exclaimed.

The doctor became quite agitated with Dad's interference. "We have to perform surgery on her right now. Right *here*."

Dad noticed an operating room nearby and asked, "What about the operating room right down the hall? Can't you at least move her there?"

"We don't have time to move her to surgery. This is an emergency!" The doctor exploded.

"Don't touch my wife! I want my family taken to another hospital," Dad exclaimed and stepped between the doctor and Mom.

At this point in the exchange, the county sheriff, who had been silently observing the situation, stepped between the two men. Dad's first thought was that he had broken a law and would be told to leave.

To Dad's surprise, the sheriff looked at the doctor and firmly said, "They will all be moved to another hospital now. Understood?"

The doctor didn't argue.

After we had been loaded into the awaiting ambulances outside, Dad glanced back through the glass doors to see the doctor laughing on the phone with his legs propped up in a chair.

The sheriff commented to Dad, "I had to get you out of there. That guy is just so drunk."

Apparently, problems had arisen at that hospital before, but the sheriff could not tell Dad to move us. Dad had to make that decision for himself. Thankfully for us, he made that decision just in time.

We later learned that the doctor on staff that night treating us had a history of problems. We found out that he had developed a substance abuse problem in college, supposedly an addiction to Demerol. At some point in time, he had even received rehabilitation treatment. The United States had refused to give him a license to practice medicine because of this problem. To get around this, he had simply gone to Latin America and obtained a license there. He was then able to practice medicine in this clinic. His family had a lot of influence, so no one questioned the man or his ability to practice medicine, even though there had been prior instances which were questionable.

In the early hours of the morning in which we arrived, it is believed that this doctor was under the influence of either alcohol or drugs. He failed to give me the standard injection for my type of spinal cord injury, which would have reduced critical swelling.

Therefore, as my spinal column began to swell, the nerves were irreparably damaged, and the result was paralysis.

The doctor would later deny he did anything wrong to any of us that morning. It bordered on insanity what happened to us at the hands of this man. As unfortunate as the lack of competent medical care had been, because he did not kill any of us that night, we could not have his medical license revoked. Years later, the doctor agreed to a settlement due to our lawsuit against him.

The ambulance into which I was put with Mom went to another local hospital. There we would be properly stabilized before being sent to Palmyra Park Hospital in Albany, Georgia. Dad and Kim were sent on to Palmyra Park in another ambulance.

Dad was not sure where Mom and I were at this point, but he was told that we would all end up at Palmyra Park Hospital eventually. He was riding in the front of the ambulance while Kim lay unconscious in the back. The driver was going extremely fast, which made Dad even more anxious. Having just been in a serious accident, Dad couldn't stand it any longer. He asked the driver to please slow down, only to be ignored. On the verge of getting physically ill, Dad again pleaded with the driver to slow down.

Finally, the driver looked at Dad and told him that if he did not get Kim to the hospital immediately, she could die—that's how serious her injuries were. Dad had no idea that things had become so critical with Kim. Without hesitation, he encouraged the driver to continue on his pace.

It became a race against time to get Kim to the hospital for the care that she needed. Unknown to Dad at that time, Mom and I were clinging to life in the other ambulance en route to Albany.

CHAPTER TWO

Background

MY FAMILY WAS LIKE MOST middle-class families living in the South during the 1980s. I grew up in a Christian home, and my parents were dedicated to raising Kim and me in a Christian environment. The majority of our childhood memories are of our lives in South Carolina. Dad was born and raised in South Carolina. Mom was born in Pennsylvania and spent most of her life in New York before moving south to attend college.

My parents met while attending Furman University in Greenville, South Carolina. My mother, Susan Ruth Matlack, was born in Philadelphia, Pennsylvania, and my father, Wayne Babb Elmore, in Laurens, South Carolina. They grew up in two completely different worlds. But as God often orchestrates things in life, they fell in love and began their life together as husband and wife in 1967. Shortly thereafter, Dad graduated, and they relocated to Cape May Courthouse, New Jersey, for my birth that summer.

Thirteen months later, on August 12, 1968, I was born. Right from the beginning, I brought excitement and–I guess you could say–a sense of urgency into their lives. My dad got the call of my impending arrival while working at a lobster house, and after

My family just prior to the accident

changing a flat tire en route to the hospital, he arrived just moments before I did.

In 1969 when I was a year old, Dad was shipped out to Vietnam to fight in the war. Mom made the decision to remain up north to have the support of her family–who had a summer home in New Jersey but lived in New York the rest of the year–during this difficult period. Determined that I wouldn't forget what Daddy looked like, she put his picture in my crib every day. I wasn't old enough to remember any of it later, but these were trying times for my parents, as they were for many families during the Vietnam War. The separation they faced as a young married couple was mirrored by many other military families across the country.

Dad wasn't sure he would make it home to see either of us again. The time ticked away as he counted several friends killed from enemy fire. A little more than a year after being shipped out, Dad finally arrived back home.

Dad had always dreamed of becoming a stockbroker. Even while in Vietnam, he slept with an economics book under his pillow as a reminder of his future plans, if he ever made it home.

Me when I was around 6 years old

After returning from Vietnam, he worked for a few different companies before accepting a job with one of the country's most well-known brokerage firms. We were living in Valley Cottage, New York, and on April 25, 1973, my little sister, Kimberly Ann Elmore, was born. Although Dad was happy in his job, he yearned to return to South Carolina.

Soon after Kim's birth, we moved back to Greenville, South Carolina so that we could live a little closer to Dad's childhood home and family. Fortunately, he was able to continue to work as a broker with the same firm while also taking night classes to complete his MBA degree at Furman. Mom, meanwhile, took a job as a physical education teacher at a nearby primary school while completing her bachelor's degree at Furman.

My school picture when I was about 8 years old

Kim and I shortly after we moved to Little Saddlebags Farm

Several years later, in 1979, we moved to a farm in Anderson County. Kim and I were elated with the spacious fields, creeks, and woods in which we'd be able to play. Dad and Mom named the farm Little Saddlebags Farm. Over time, we got horses and cows. There were not many neighbors close by, but we were perfectly happy to entertain each other.

Within a couple of years, my parents were able to build a new house on the property, and we moved from the original farmhouse. Our new home was bigger, and Kim and I each finally had our own rooms.

As Kim and I grew up, our interests changed, and we did not do as many things together. My passions were fishing and horses, while Kim wanted to spend her time doing other things.

We fought and argued, but deep down, we really loved and supported each other.

Our personalities were very different from the beginning. Kim was a risk taker. She was willing to take chances and test her boundaries. I was the opposite—cautious and obeying any rules. Kim and I would both rebel in our own ways as we went through adolescence. She was blatant and external with her actions. I was more subtle and internalized my feelings.

I remember one time in particular when Kim was in elementary school. While swinging on swings at the playground, she decided to jump out in mid-air. The problem was that her arms got stuck. She ended up with two broken arms! She was quite pitiful-looking with those two casts on, but she did seem to savor the attention.

Our family attended Beaverdam Baptist Church near Anderson. It was a small country church not far from our home. I was baptized at Beaverdam and learned a lot about who God was through Bible study and my excellent teachers. These were happy years for us girls, filled with wonderful memories. Mom and Dad saw to it that we were active in the local church.

During these younger years, I developed a real passion for music, and I loved to sing, so I joined the youth choir. Occasionally, I was even able to sing solos. I was comfortable on stage because I had been performing since the third grade. This was an area I excelled in, and it gave me self-confidence. I especially enjoyed singing with my peers at church.

Although I had a lot of head knowledge, was baptized, and went to church several times a week, part of me did not want to let Jesus be on the throne of my heart. Deep down, I was self-centered.

My 4th grade class with Mrs. Galloway

I didn't want to care about what God thought about my life during the week. Even so, there were several people at Beaverdam who had a significant impact on my life spiritually. I have many fond memories from my childhood of attending vacation Bible school, participating in Baptist mission groups like Girls in Action (GAs) and Acteens, and enjoying numerous outings with my friends there. My spiritual foundation was being formed during those early years.

As a teen, I joined the ladies' softball team at Beaverdam and played alongside my mother. I was not as athletic as some, but I really enjoyed playing. My most memorable game was when I hit a line drive along right field. It was my first and only home run! It was so exciting to be a part of Beaverdam and represent them on the ball field. This church family truly was our extended family and loved us dearly. I learned later the depth and significance of this connection.

Kim and I attended Palmetto Middle School in the small town of Williamston, located east of Anderson. Mom taught physical education at the school. It was difficult being a teacher's kid because the other kids would pick on me. It didn't help that they also found me unattractive with my freckles, red hair, and bucked teeth. Kids tend to be mean sometimes, so I didn't have very good self-esteem in regards to my appearance.

I did excel academically and was a good student. I worked hard to become a better athlete. I enjoyed playing basketball. Though I struggled, I did make the C-Team basketball team in the seventh grade. I didn't get to play much my first two years

Me with my gymnastics team at Palmetto Middle School during a pep rally

Me striking a pose at gymnastics camp at Furman University

Me with my JV basketball team

because I wasn't as good as the other girls on the team. However, I remember one time I did get to play and actually made a basket. I was ecstatic. I immediately looked at Mom who was helping at the scoreboard and yelled, "It went in!" Everyone laughed. I didn't care. I was proud of my accomplishment. I wanted to be a better player, so I even went to summer basketball camps and practiced continuously with my basketball goal at home.

At the beginning of my ninth grade year, I finally made it to the first string of the JV team. I was so excited about the up-coming season. Unfortunately, those two points I made in the previous season were the only points I would ever make for my school's JV basketball team.

Another great passion, besides music, was my love for horses. It didn't matter if I were riding, brushing, or feeding them, I enjoyed horses. I spent most of my time during the summers in the barn or out in the pastures on horseback. We raised a beautiful little Appaloosa filly, Pebbles, and she was such a joy to ride. She became my sole responsibility.

I was a member of a local pony club and occasionally went on outings with them. Just prior to the accident, I had started jumping and working on dressage to move up in my riding skills rating so that I could begin competing.

I had absolutely no fear when it came to horses, especially with Pebbles. We had an incredible connection between us. I understood her, and she seemed to understand me. We had many adventures together, and I learned a lot about responsibility through taking care of her and all of my tackle. I considered her one of my dearest friends. I also spent a lot of time fishing in our pond on the farm, and Pebbles would often graze near me as I fished. She loved to walk in the pond and paw at the water during the summer to cool herself off.

My first and only dressage competition with my horse, Pebbles.

When I began high school in the fall of 1982, I was very anxious about being in with all the "big" kids. It was different from middle school. Being at the bottom of the totem pole was very intimidating. I was still kind of scrawny and had nicknames like Howdy Doody, Big Red, and Firetruck because of all my freckles, bucked teeth, and red hair. The taunting was only in jest, but at the age of 14, I found that it wasn't always easy to take and further eroded my self-esteem at this critical time in my life.

The adjustment to being a high school freshman was not an easy one, but I was beginning to feel comfortable as the first quarter came to an end. I had learned my way around the school and knew what the teachers expected of me. When I discovered a Christian group of students who met and had Bible studies together during the week, I joined them. I felt comfortable with them since many of them also attended Beaverdam. This

Me horseback riding on our farm

Christian Student Union led a devotion time over the intercom in the mornings at school. Obviously, this was years before God was taken out of school.

My life was very good, and to the extent that any teenager can, I appreciated it. I had hopes and dreams of what my life was going to be like. As far as I could see, the sky was the limit. My ambitions of becoming a singer and excelling in anything else I chose to do were achievable goals. My parents raised me to have a positive and ambitious outlook. Despite living in a small-town environment, there was never a question of whether I would go to college, only where.

As I've said, my life and my family's lives were very similar to other rural families in the South. Both of my parents worked, we attended church and school, and we enjoyed many extracurricular activities. Our vacations often included visiting family, so the Thanksgiving trip to Florida was just one of several we had taken through the years.

But the balance in our lives changed dramatically after the accident. The challenges we faced in the following years were immeasurable and at times seemed unconquerable. If not for the faith we possessed and the closeness of our family, we very well might have given up. We were four very different individuals with strong constitutions and distinctive personalities, but that horrendous night in Georgia brought us together in a way we had never before experienced.

CHAPTER THREE

Survival and Stability

THE AMBULANCE CARRYING KIM AND Dad arrived at Palmyra Park Hospital in Albany, Georgia, in the early morning hours of Thanksgiving Day. Mom and I arrived shortly thereafter. Despite his hand injuries sustained from trying to break the camper windows, Dad had yet to receive medical treatment himself. It frankly had not registered with him that he might have been injured. He was desperately trying to hold on to the rest of us. Dad had been told upon arrival in Albany that he would be very fortunate if *any* of us survived. The seriousness of our injuries and the delays in receiving competent medical care had placed us in even more jeopardy.

I awoke in the emergency room of Palmyra Park Hospital. The back of my head was being shaved in order to stitch a laceration. As the nurses removed my jewelry and began cutting off my clothing, I asked them where I was. They calmly explained to me that I had been in a serious car accident and I was in the emergency room at Palmyra. They assured me everything would be okay before I promptly lost consciousness again.

Several hours later, Kim and I were placed in the surgical intensive care unit (SICU) after being stabilized in the emergency room. We were put beside each other on Stryker Frames, a bed that sandwiches a patient so he or she can be flipped from one side to the other at certain intervals. This helps to prevent pressure sores from developing. Due to the nature of our spinal injuries, we both required this type of a bed.

I still was not able to remain conscious for very long periods of time. I did not yet understand the magnitude of my circumstances. The first familiar face I remember seeing was Uncle Ty from Florida. Dad had called him, and he had driven at top speed to get to Albany. Although Uncle Ty smiled at me and tried to be encouraging, I saw fear and worry on his face. He had something for me, he said. From behind his back he brought an adorable yellow teddy bear with white markings. I decided to name him Old Yeller, even though I had never actually read the book or seen the movie. Uncle Ty then presented me with his second "prize," a tube of bright pink lipstick! Being a bachelor, he didn't even know how to open it. I could not help but chuckle as I watched him twist the tube without taking off the lid. We both grinned at the then-distorted smudge of pink stuck to the inside of the lid. There was no doubt in my mind—Uncle Ty loved us so much.

Most of the time, our hospital stay was more difficult. One of the times I awoke, I looked across the SICU and saw Mom unconscious in her hospital bed. Dad was sitting at her side holding her hand. He looked incredibly sad. The doctors really had no idea

what was wrong with Mom or how long she would be unconscious. It had been approximately 24 hours since the collision.

The nurses came in at this point and began to roll my bed out
of the SICU to take me to surgery. I stopped them and asked to
be rolled next to my little sister. I looked at Kim and tried to be
strong because I could see that she was very scared. Feeling bad
for the times we had fought, I apologized. I told her that I loved
her more than anything in the world. Our hands were locked
together, and we held on tightly, afraid to let go. As we did, we
both broke down in tears. As the nurses began to roll me away,
I told Kim to take care of Mom and Dad because I didn't know
if I would be coming back or not. I sobbed as I was rolled down
the hall.

Everything in my mind was still a jumble. I did not understand that my overall medical condition had stabilized. The critical period had actually passed.

I was taken to surgery to reconstruct the left side of my face.
My nose had been broken in the accident, my left cheekbone
shattered, and my left eye had come out of its socket. During this
surgery, a wire mesh was placed where my cheekbone had been,
and everything else was repaired as best as it could be.

The doctors told Dad that I would probably never see out of
my left eye again due to the trauma it had endured. Sometime
after the surgery, I did regain vision in my left eye—only it was
inverted! Everything I looked at with my left eye was upside
down. The doctors took this as a good sign and said that it might
slowly correct itself. It did!

A few days later, I had surgery to repair my spine. It had been crushed at levels T-11 and T-12, leaving me completely paralyzed from the waist down. The doctors placed two Harrington rods in my back, one on each side of my spinal cord, to stabilize it while it healed. Part of my left hip was also removed to provide extra support for my spine, so I had two significant incisions— one the entire length of my back and another about six inches long just over my left hip.

Because I already had major issues with self-esteem, looking in the mirror at my damaged face was not high on my list of priorities at this point. I was terribly afraid of what I might see. At the same time, I was in denial that my face could possibly look that bad. But one day, a young boy about my age walked past my bed to visit his grandmother who was across the SICU from me. I smiled real big as he passed by, fluttering whatever eyelashes I had left, hoping to catch his attention. To my horror, he stopped abruptly, his jaw dropped, and he turned pale. After what seemed like an eternity, he hurried on without smiling or speaking. It was then that I realized how terrible I probably looked.

I was too devastated to tell anyone about this experience. I was determined to look at my face and see for myself what I looked like. Soon afterward, one of Mom's good friends came to visit us. I asked her if she could bring me a mirror. She hesitated and said she wasn't sure that was such a good idea, but I insisted. It was a small mirror she handed me, but it reflected the reality of my injuries in a huge way.

As I hesitantly looked into the reflection, I was devastated. No wonder that young boy had turned away as if he had seen a monster. He had! Aside from my cuts, bruises, and dried blood, my face was red and puffy due to an allergic reaction to a medication. At that moment, I truly lost all hope. I had no desire to live.

My despair was overwhelming. I would be an outcast—a cripple! Thrown into a spiral of depressive thoughts, I knew I could not go on. It had to end. There was only one way out—I had to kill myself. Devising a plan that I thought would solve everything, I began saving my oral medication gradually so no one would notice. I would hide a pill under my tongue and then take it out and hide it when no one was around. Once I had enough pills, I would overdose on them. In the midst of my confusion, though, there was the tiniest glimmer of light. Even though I was afraid of living, I was even more afraid of dying. The things that I had learned in Sunday school started coming back to me. My teachers and pastor taught me that God was bigger than anything and that He was always with me. Was He with me right now? I wanted to know. More importantly, I needed to know.

I couldn't bother Dad because he was tending to Mom and wondering if she would ever be the same again. I needed someone—and that someone was God! I cried out to Him in despair. If He was really there, like everyone had told me He was, then I needed to feel His presence. I needed to feel His comfort and peace. I had come to the end of myself. I have heard others say, "I had nowhere to look but up." And that's exactly what God was waiting for…and that is exactly where God met me.

I felt a Power, much larger and stronger than I ever could have imagined, come over me. God gave me the peace, hope, physical strength, and determination that I needed to go on. My little belief system that nothing bad would ever happen to someone like me had disintegrated—it had been shattered. Not only *can* bad things happen to good, young, or innocent people, they *do*. And it had happened to me. I had to deal with this reality, but I did not have to deal with it alone.

I had a lifeline. There is a great truth here that many people rail against in the midst of adversity. It's one that some never understand or won't accept. Life is hard, but God is good! I finally got it. God sent His Son, Jesus Christ, to die for my sins over two thousand years ago. At that moment in my hospital bed, He came into my heart as I confessed my weakness and my need for Him. He didn't put me on hold, and He didn't put me on a waiting list. God, in His mercy, was ready and waiting to comfort me right then. It was at that point in my life that I knew I was a Christian. I would not attempt to overdose on those few pills that I had stashed away.

I didn't know whether or not God would choose to heal me, but I knew beyond a shadow of a doubt that no matter what, He would be *with* me. He would never leave me nor forsake me (Hebrews 13:5). I could do all things through Christ who would strengthen me (Philippians 4:13). They were more than words on a page. I experienced them; they became personal to me. That was all the comfort I needed.

There were countless people who offered comfort to my family. The people of Albany were so kind. They didn't even know us, and yet they brought us cards, gifts, food, and flowers. They had heard or read in the newspaper about our accident and felt sympathy for our whole family. Kim and I could not have many visitors in the SICU, but we did get to read the cards and letters brought in bags each day. It was kind of fun getting all of that attention, almost like we were famous or something. The Lord really used those people to not only minister to my family but to encourage us, as well.

One particular priest from a local church was allowed to visit on a regular basis. He would come and read the Bible to me. I would always have him read Philippians chapter four because it had become such an encouragement to me. Many other area churches reached out, as well, and many people prayed. I came to believe in the power of prayer. My real spiritual journey had begun.

Before leaving Albany, the nurses in the emergency room got together and bought Kim and me original Cabbage Patch dolls. Kim's had blonde hair with blue eyes, and mine had red hair with green eyes. I named mine Nancy after one of my best friends back home. We became very close to all of the nurses during our stay. Two of our favorites were Robin and Lisa, who were our primary nurses during the days in SICU.

I remember one day when Robin had to replace my IV. I had always hated needles, but I had gotten paranoid of IVs. I began to cry because she had to stick me several times to find a vein. She began crying too and finally had to get someone else to insert it.

Kim was more of a clown. One night, without anyone prompting her to do so, she decided to rip all of her wires off to see what would happen. Several little alarms started going off, and nurses came scrambling to check on her. She got the biggest kick out of that. We still laugh about that to this day.

One of the coolest things we were given were prism glasses so we could watch television as we lay on our beds. That helped to keep us occupied and out of mischief. By that time, we were recovering well and did not require as much attention. We became quite creative in both positions on the Stryker Frame, too. When we were facing up, we would watch television, eat, or read. Face down, we would hang our arms down and do crafts like clay modeling or cross-stitch, play games like backgammon, or read our many cards. At times, the nurses would even play games with us or paint our fingernails. They were all such wonderful people. They gave me such an appreciation for people in the medical field. I still have tremendous respect for them.

One of my more horrible memories was when Kim had to have a medical device called a "halo" put on to stabilize her neck while we were in SICU. The procedure entailed drilling four holes into Kim's skull to mount this steel structure to her head. It would act as a brace to protect her neck from further injury until the cervical vertebrae had grown back together properly. For whatever reason, the doctors decided to do the procedure right there in the SICU.

The doctors gave Kim several doses of anesthesia in hopes of putting her under for the ordeal. It was crucial that the halo be put on at that time, so they proceeded even though the anesthesia was not having the desired effect on Kim. They had given her the maximum dose. She had gotten so anxious about the whole procedure that she had literally blocked the effect of the medicine. I can still hear her blood-curdling screams as they drilled the four holes into her skull, two on each side of her forehead and two on the back of her head. It was horrible hearing her writhe in pain and scream like that. I cried and begged the nurses to move me toward Kim to comfort her, but they would not. They simply drew the curtain around my bed and tried their best to distract me.

Dad was outside the SICU doors with Mom's dad, listening to Kim's cries, but they were not allowed in, either. After the painful ordeal was over, it was then that Kim slept. The medication finally had the desired effect, and her body was exhausted. She did not wake up for two days.

I was emotionally drained—it felt as if every bit of life had come out of me. I had never cried so hard and so long in my life as I did the day that happened. Furthermore, I didn't fully grasp the magnitude of the whole string of events happening to my family. That would take years to process. In the midst of the pain and suffering, it was more about survival than anything else. Kim and I had to survive. This aspect of our personalities came out very prominently during this tragedy. We had to have strong wills if we were going to make it, although the journey that lay ahead for each of us was very different.

Kim had to wear the halo for six months. Her neck had been broken at a very critical level. It was very unusual for someone with her injury to have lived at all—much less without paralysis. The doctors attributed it to the fact that she was so young and her bones were still developing. They said she should have a full recovery and would appear normal when the halo was removed.

"Enough Pain For A Lifetime!"

Family Faces Long Road To Recovery

by Beth Rogers

On November 24, 1982, Laurie and Kim Elmore were looking forward to an autumn vacation and a trip to the new Epcot Center at Florida's Walt Disney World.

Twenty-four hours later, on Thanksgiving Day, both Laurie and Kim and their parents became statistics -- four of thousands of persons tragically scarred by alcohol-related automobile accidents every year.

This Williamston family is now trying to recover from the grinding crash of that night -- both physically and emotionally. Laurie is in a wheelchair and her sister is in "halo cast," a type of neck brace which prevents her from moving her broken neck.

Less than three months since the accident, Laurie says she has a message for the people around her. What follows is her own account of what happened on Thanksgiving, 1982, in a personal letter to the President of the United States:

"Dear President Reagan,

"My name is Laurie Emore and I am 14 years old. I am a paraplegic. My family and I were traveling to Florida for a Thanksgiving vacation Nov. 25, '82, about 2:00 a.m. when we were hit by a drunk head-on. We were traveling in a Chevrolet pickup truck pulling a trailer load of about 100 Christmas trees to sell at my uncle's nursery shop in Florida. My nine-year-old sister and I were asleep in the rear of the truck. My mother and father were in the cab. My mother was asleep and my father was driving.

"The man that hit us was driving a pickup truck, also. He had four other family members with him in his vehicle.

"The accident occurred when the man, traveling in the opposite highway, crossed the median and came swerving and aiming directly at us, no matter which way my father turned to avoid him. In a last effort to save our family, my father hit the brakes. The man hit us head-on with an impact of 90 mph. He was traveling at 60mph and we were traveling at 30 mph.

"The impact was so great it brought the engine of our vehicle into the seat of the cab. My mother was left unconscious. My sister was left with a broken neck which easily could have killed her. I awoke at the sound of the brakes, and by lifting my head upward I was thrown to the back of the cab then thrown into the camper top, leaving an imprint of my body.

"I remember hearing my father calling to me when it was over, then I fell unconscious. My back was broken in two places along with my nose and my cheekbone. My left eye was literally hanging out.

"This accident would not have happened if the other driver had not been drunk. (This was not the first time he had been caught drunk driving.)

"The first hospital we were taken to the doctor was drunk! He tried to perform open heart surgery on my mother's

(Continued on Page 10)

Back Home

Laurie and Kim Elmore are both glad to be back home. "There's no place like home and being with my family and friends," said Kim. (Photo by Beth Rogers)

Story which was printed about our family's accident in the Williamston Journal shortly after the accident

Long Road . . .

(Continued from Page 1)

stomach out in the corridor, and also made an effort to sit my sister up with a broken neck. Meanwhile, he left me in an isolated room for three hours before I received any attention. Thanks to the sheriff who was on the scene of the accident, we were then taken to three more hospitals before being admitted to Palmyra Park Hospital in Albany, Georgia. There, later that morning, I received surgery on my back. By placing a Herringbone Rod in my back to support the broken parts, the doctors saved my life. Six days later I received plastic surgery on my left eye, cheekbone, and my nose.

"My family and I were at this hospital for three weeks and three days.

"Now my family is back home and I am at Roger C. Peace Rehabilitation Hospital in Greenville, S.C. Here, I am recovering from my back injury.

"President Reagan, the reason I wrote this letter is because I believe there should be stiffer penalties toward drunk driving. I also believe any drunk driver that kills or even injures an innocent person should be confined to prison for at least five years.

"As for the drunk doctor, I believe he should have his license for practicing medicine taken away.

"I hope that some action will be taken against drunk drivers so that other innocent people will not have to go through what I have endured.

"It would really mean a lot to me if you wrote back to let me know what you think about this incident and, if any, what actions shall be taken against drunk drivers. I still have some years to go, President Reagan, but I sure have endured enough pain for a lifetime!

"Sincerely, Laurie Elmore"

Things around the Elmore household have changed since the accident. Laurie certainly isn't as mobile as she used to be, and the Elmores are remodeling their home to accommodate a wheelchair. They have replaced the steps with ramps and are now in the process of having a special bathroom built for Laurie.

Kim hopes to have her cast removed in about six weeks. Doctors hope there will be no serious long-term physical complications for her.

Their mother, a physical education teacher, now suffers a slight loss of physical coordination.

Physcial scars, emotional scars . . .

And what of the man who caused it all? What happened to the drunk driver in that accident? The Elmores were denied that information about the man who — they were told it would be a "violation of his civil rights."

The doctor at the Georgia hospital told Laurie she would not be able to walk again. But after spending four weeks at the Roger C. Peace Institute in Greenville, Laurie's doctors feel that, in time, she may be able to walk again with the aid of a walker. Laurie says she will someday walk without the help of a walker.

The Elmores say they are taking life "one day at a time" now. They feel fortunate to be alive and say they are very thankful for all the help they received from friends in the community.

"There's no place like home and being with my family and friends," said Kim.

The family expressed a special thanks to the Williamston Rescue Squad for coming to Georgia and bringing them home.

Although the man who crashed into the Elmores' truck that night was drunk, alcohol is not the culprit.

The culprit is the person who takes the drink and then climbs in behind the wheel of his car, pompously thinking that he can "handle" it.

The culprits are also those of us who choose to ignore the problem and do nothing about it.

Laurie Elmore thinks something ought to be done. What does it take to convince the rest of us?

Three weeks after arriving in Albany, I was moved to a private room. Kim had been moved shortly before me. Now I was expected to try to sit up for a certain amount of time each day to regain my strength. It was amazing how weak I felt. I would sit up in my bed for a few minutes, get nauseated, and then vomit. It was hard to imagine that I would ever be normal again.

I finally got the strength to sit up in a wheelchair long enough to be rolled outside. My granddad, who had gotten an apartment temporarily in Albany, wheeled me out for the first time. The world looked so different from the way I remembered it. The trees were so much more beautiful, the flowers so delicate, and the sky so blue. There was a gentle breeze, and I could smell the freshly cut grass as soon as the automatic doors opened to the hospital. The world had not changed during those few weeks of my being bedridden, but my attitude and appreciation of it had. I was experiencing it in a whole new, wonderful way.

God had given me a new appreciation for life. Everything was beautiful! He made such a wonderful world, and I had been given another opportunity to experience it. However, sitting up for even that short period of time, and the excitement from all that I had taken in, left me exhausted. My granddad wheeled me back up to my room.

A few days later, on December 19, 1982, the doctor who performed my back surgery came to see me. He removed some sixty staples from the long incision on my back—each one feeling like a bee sting as it came out. I was then fitted for a back brace that I would have to wear for six months to allow my spine to regain its strength. He told me that my back had been broken at levels T-11 and T-12 and that I would be paralyzed from the waist down for the rest of my life. He said there was no hope of my ever walking or running, let alone playing basketball or horseback riding again.

As devastating as this news should have been, remarkably, it wasn't. I told him that I appreciated his being honest with me and telling me what he was required to, but the Lord *could* heal me if He *chose* to because He alone is the Great Physician. The doctor looked at me sympathetically and tried to smile before walking away. I knew he didn't believe me, but that didn't matter. I found out later that he was an atheist, and I have often wondered if any of my words penetrated his heart.

Of course, I wanted to be completely whole again, but I had no guarantee of that. I knew that I would have to do the best I could at therapy and trust God with my life, whether I lived in a wheelchair or not. That much I did know for certain. I clung to that belief through the difficult months that lay ahead. Naturally, I prayed that God would heal me, too.

Before Christmas, after spending almost a month in the Albany hospital, Kim and I were transported via ambulance to Roger C. Peace Rehabilitation Hospital in Greenville, South Carolina. Our hometown of Williamston had volunteered to send one of its ambulances to transport us. The people of Williamston had been very supportive of my family. They had sent numerous cards over the weeks during our stay in Albany. They continued to do so for many more months. They had been so faithful in reminding us of home and praying diligently for our family.

I remember the day and the trip home very vividly. Upon our arrival at the rehabilitation hospital, Kim was examined. She did not require any therapy, so she was able to go home. I was a bit envious because I would have to stay for three months and be taught how to live with a disability—life in a wheelchair. Kim was excited, but it was a tremendous letdown for me because I was looking forward to our being together in this strange, new place.

I was weak from the journey in the ambulance and from being moved around so much that I couldn't really focus on my emotions. Exhaustion was setting in, but I was thrilled when the nurses said they were going to give me a shower. I hadn't had one since the accident! I had only been given sponge baths in my bed. There at Roger C. Peace, I was put on a stainless steel bed and rolled into a huge shower area.

When the nurses removed my back brace, there was a tremendous stench. It had not been removed since it had been put on me in Albany, and it had gotten quite nasty. I guess they didn't know or didn't think to put a T-shirt under the brace, and it was against my bare skin. That was one of the best showers I have ever had in my life! I will never take being clean for granted ever again.

That first night was very difficult as I lay in my bed trying to go to sleep in a new place. I had grown accustomed to my parents not being there, but at least Kim had been with me. Now she wasn't there. I knew I would wake up the next morning physically alone. The loneliness was almost unbearable. For the first time in my life, I was completely dependent on God for comfort. Being a mere child, I had no way of knowing that the pain and heartache I had already been through was only the beginning. There would be many more days of despair and loneliness ahead for me.

Chapter Four

Rehab

Upon my arrival at Roger C. Peace, my parents and Kim toured the hospital facility with me. It was very overwhelming. Feelings of sadness and anxiety filled me as we were escorted through the various therapy divisions. I could hardly focus as the staff told us about the physical, occupational, and recreational regimens. As they explained the rules, I knew my stay was going to be a real challenge physically.

Waking up alone on Christmas morning was probably the lowest point I had while at Roger C. Peace. I knew that God was with me, but my family wasn't. They promised me they would arrive as early as possible, but it wasn't the same as waking up at home. Christmas morning had always been a special time at our house.

Kim and I would jump out of bed and race into the living room to see what was in our stockings and open tons of presents. I had memories of laughing, eating M&Ms for breakfast, seeing all of my cousins, aunts, uncles, and grandparents, and having a big meal together. But instead, there was silence—deafening, depressing silence.

This special day began no differently than any other day. I cried, but not where anyone could see me. I didn't want the nurses or anyone to know how much it hurt, though I'm sure they suspected. I wanted to be happy and positive, but I just couldn't be. The same dark cloud of despair hovered over me that had led me to almost attempt suicide in Albany. I never wanted to experience that again, and I refused to give in to it.

I rolled my wheelchair downstairs to the main entrance to wait for my family to arrive. It seemed an eternity as I watched other happy families come through those automatic doors. Each person I saw who wasn't there for me was like a knife into my heart. That huge lump stayed in my throat when I tried to smile at the people who walked past me. I didn't want to cry in front of any one of them. I had to be strong.

Then, finally I caught a glimpse of <u>my</u> family. *Now* it was Christmas! It really did not matter that we spent it in a hospital room with a tiny mantle-sized Christmas tree. All that mattered was that my family was with me. My sadness evaporated into overwhelming joy.

My parents gave me several Aigner items that Christmas because that was the popular clothing and accessory name brand at that time. They presented me with a beautiful Aigner leather coat, shoes, a belt, and a purse. I still have that coat because it is a reminder of my most difficult Christmas. I never want to take that experience for granted. As much as I hated being away from home, I learned that year that Christmas could be celebrated wherever I was. I also realized how precious family was.

The staff at the hospital was kind but also very firm. From the beginning, they pushed me to do things on my own. This was frustrating for me because I was so physically weak. I will never forget one of the first mornings there; a nurse came in and put my clothes on the foot of the bed. She said something to the effect of, "Do your best to dress yourself." I could barely sit up in the bed! The mere *thought* of putting pants on, much less socks, overwhelmed me. It was a terrible feeling to be completely alone, no family or friends, and to be asked to accomplish such a seemingly impossible, almost monumental task. I did want to be independent, even though I really did not grasp the complete depth of the concept at that point. Fortunately for me, the highly skilled staff at Roger C. Peace was determined to make me independent—and I needed to be pushed.

The first several days in rehab were grueling because of all the tests I needed. One of the tests was a total body X-ray with contrast dye to ensure I didn't have any internal damage that may have been previously undetected in Albany. Another test that was extremely painful was done on my kidneys and bladder to test their capacity, I believe. I was warned the pain would be similar to birth pains. Telling this to a fourteen-year-old will definitely keep her from wanting to have children. They were right—I felt as though I were being tortured, and it was a very horrible experience.

My saddest moments were definitely in the mornings when I first awakened. Each day the reality of my situation, being alone, struck me anew. Having to eat in the community dining hall instead of at my kitchen table was difficult because it forced me to interact with other patients, and sometimes I didn't feel like talking. I didn't think anyone would understand me. I still couldn't grasp that other patients had similar stories to mine.

Physical therapy was grueling. Although I had some form of therapy every day, I had physical therapy daily. My physical therapist, Diana, was awesome because she was also fun. She turned out to be a great motivator and pushed me, but she was also encouraging and didn't make me feel bad about myself. Our personalities clicked right from the beginning. Her goal was to make me independent so I did not have to depend upon anyone for anything.

Most of the time Diana would get me out on a mat that was on a kind of ledge or bench, and then she would stretch my muscles with different exercises. An embarrassing incident happened one day while Diana was stretching my muscles. She accidentally pushed on my bladder, and I had an accident on the mat. I was so embarrassed and ashamed at my lack of control, but this instance proved to be a bonding experience for us.

Diana eventually taught me how to get up on all fours and try to keep my balance and not fall over. That was incredibly difficult since I was paralyzed, but I had to learn to manipulate my legs. I couldn't just let them be dead weight. I had to learn to adjust my body in ways so that I could use the weight of my legs to my advantage, whether transporting from wheelchair to bench, wheelchair to potty seat or tub, or wheelchair to vehicle and vice versa. Rehab was very difficult work, but I really trusted Diana.

I lifted weights with my arms to make them stronger since I was using them more to get around. Diana taught me how to go up and down ramps and how to pop wheelies so that I could get in and out of public places. At the time, most public places did not have wheelchair access, so this was a very important skill to perfect. Handicap access wouldn't become law until years later. I also learned how to fall out of my wheelchair without hurting myself and how to get myself back in. This was scary but necessary—again, an emphasis upon independence.

Transferring from different positions would have been very difficult without a sliding board. It was one of the first things I made in occupational therapy, and it became an integral part of my physical therapy. Each of us personalized our boards by wood-burning and shellacking them. I used my board to get in and out of the car; therefore, I took it with me wherever I went. I also used it to get onto the mat in physical therapy.

Other times in physical therapy, we had fun. We used medicine balls that were five to ten pounds each and threw them to others in a group. It really develops balance because once you throw the ball, you've got to sit upright and not fall over. I eventually got strong enough to knock the therapist off her seat, which I thought was quite the accomplishment! Even the therapists laughed.

My biggest accomplishment in physical therapy was also my scariest. Diana took me to a flight of stairs and wanted me to go up and come back down in my wheelchair by myself. She stressed the fact that, although there might be someone around to help me, I couldn't depend on that. In my mind, I still didn't believe I would always be in a wheelchair. Of course, everyone felt that way in rehab. Rarely does one accept the initial diagnosis of paralysis. But basically, it scared me to even think of going up those stairs and back down.

I tried to explain that I had no intention of ever going up and down a flight of stairs by myself, but Diana stressed I was missing the point. My chair had to become part of who I was. I had to be able to function with it. I did make it all the way up the flight of stairs and back down, but this was one exercise I did only in rehab with Diana's assistance. I didn't attempt it again.

During the months of physical therapy, Diana would put me up on my feet at the end of the sessions. I would stand between parallel bars for a period of time, sometimes only for a few minutes. In time, I regained my strength and eventually began getting some of the feeling back below my waist. It was a gradual process. When I began having feeling in my thighs again, I was then able to start exercising my quadriceps.

Diana eventually put me in braces that fit from my waist down. They were metal with leather straps that tied the braces to my legs. I would practice standing with my balance and getting the feel of them. I never regained the feeling below my knees, but I did learn to use crutches in rehab and begin to take steps. Granddaddy Matlack happened to be there when I took my first step, which was really special for me. We had always had a close relationship.

As the therapy progressed, I graduated to AFOs (leg braces) and forearm crutches. The intensity of the work that went behind all that was amazing. In one sense the progress was incredibly slow, but in another sense the progress was encouraging, no matter how small the gains. I never did regain the use of my hamstrings and remained paralyzed in my buttocks, down the backs of my legs, and completely from the knees down. I had drop foot since I had no muscle or movement control in my lower extremities. It was, therefore, necessary for me to always wear AFOs if I was going to walk again.

I also learned to cook from the wheelchair in occupational therapy. I had a plastic tray that was attached with Velcro to my wheelchair arms. It provided a large work area to place a mixing bowl and ingredients that I could work with. The therapist taught me to use a grabber so I could reach up into cabinets or get items out of the refrigerator. It brought everything within arm's reach and, once again, allowed me to be independent. To graduate from that particular task in OT, I had to use my grabber to pick up a dime, which is extremely difficult, but eventually I did it.

Recreational therapy was the "fun" therapy. We didn't consider what we were doing to be work. We learned how to do things like play basketball. Our therapists also took us off campus from the hospital into public places, which was scary at first. Riding in the van strapped in a wheelchair was unnerving. You don't feel as secure as you do in a regular seat. It didn't help that the first time out, our driver drove recklessly and fast. He eventually lost his job because of his driving skills, or lack thereof, so I was told.

Recreational therapists took us to the movies, to restaurants, and to the mall, anywhere we could practice our skills from PT. I remember the first time pulling up in the van to a movie theater and seeing a line to the ticket counter going all the way down the sidewalk, and of course, where did we have to park? Right there at the door. They let all of us "cripples" out in our wheelchairs. We were an assortment of young and old alike, those who had been victims of accidents, strokes, a variety of injuries. We felt like we were from the funny farm the way people stared at us. I'm sure in our minds the stares were probably exaggerated, but those teenagers were my peers. It was absolutely terrible because I still had a bald spot on the crown of my head with all the little hairs of new growth sticking up out of it. I still was very self-conscious about the way I looked.

But the purpose of the recreational therapy was to bring us out into the world and then bring us back into the safety and security of the hospital to regroup and talk about our feelings. These were my first experiences with "group therapy." The outings were an opportunity to put our therapy into practice, see how we could function, and grow accustomed to how people would respond to us. However, the outings were probably the worst part of therapy.

One of the integral parts of my stay was the unofficial counseling and group therapy. At first, I rejected the notion of group therapy because I didn't think anyone could possibly understand what I was going through. I was lonely, and I hated the loneliness, but I didn't want to be around anybody else who reflected what I was struggling with. Every time I looked at somebody else in a wheelchair, I was thinking, "that's what I am," and I didn't want to accept that. Everybody else was older than I was, too.

As I grew to accept my situation, I eventually began to make friends. One such friend was a college student. She had been dancing at a party, and her partner dipped her back and dropped her accidentally. She landed on her head and broke her neck, permanently paralyzing her from the neck down. She was incredibly bitter and didn't want anyone to come see her. I was one of the only people she would talk to. It was really, really sad. She was so angry. I could not relate to her anger.

There was also a young man who was in his thirties; he had been hunting and fell out of a tree stand. He landed on a tree and broke his back, leaving him paralyzed. He had a wife and children at home.

Then there was an elderly man we called Pluto. He was bald and legally blind. Toward the end of my stay, I found so much joy doing things for other patients, so I would sing to him. I also read Scripture to Pluto since he couldn't see. We developed really neat friendships with each other on our floor.

Going to group therapy turned out to be a good thing. It wasn't anything like what I had imagined it to be. It was a place to talk about my fears, anxieties, and anything that had to do with my new life with a disability and how I was going to manage in the world. We could ask questions. We also had fun with some of the questions and topics that were brought up, subjects you couldn't talk about with other people. I dealt with many issues during those months of group therapy, but most importantly, I strengthened my relationship with the Lord.

Visiting time was special too. I often had many visitors, usually friends from high school. They didn't make me feel uneasy by staring at me. They accepted me. They were very supportive and sent many cards and letters. My basketball team visited, which was particularly special. I had several guy friends who called or came by in a platonic way. I didn't even think about anything else. I couldn't. The fact that they cared meant so much to me because they were true friends.

The day came when I was discharged and allowed to go home. I returned for outpatient therapy for several months before being completely discharged. Therapy continued to be challenging and left me exhausted. There were days I was so exhausted that I didn't want to get out of bed, but my craving for independence motivated me. I didn't want anybody to dress me. I wanted to be able to get up, put my clothes on, transfer myself into the chair, do my hair and makeup, and not have anybody do these things for me. And in time, I actually began to feel fairly independent.

I think the most difficult situation for me, once I was discharged, was seeing other people and dealing with their reactions. I'm sure it goes back to my age at the time of the accident. In the months ahead, I would return to my old life and school, but I would never be the same. The girl who had climbed into the back of that camper truck with her little sister months before no longer existed. It would be years before I came close to regaining any semblance of my former life.

As a teenager, I was finding myself. What differentiated me from my peers was that I went through this maturity process and change while also dealing with extreme adversity. My personal, internal strength revealed itself in my Christian faith. I knew who I was in Christ, and that foundation sustained me.

Rt. 1, Box 384
Williamston S.C.
29697
January 10, 83'

-1-

President Ronald Reagan
White House
Washington D.C.

Dear President Reagan,
    My name is Laurie Elmore
and I am 14 years old. I am
a paraplegic. My family and
I were traveling to Florida
for a Thanksgiving vacation
Nov. 26, 82' about 2:00 A.M. when
we were hit by a drunk
head-on. we were traveling in
a Chevrolet pickup truck pulling a trailer load of about 100
Christmas trees to sell at my
uncles nursery shop in Florida.
My nine year old sister and
I were asleep in the rear of
the truck. My mother and father
were in the cab. My mother was
asleep and my father was driving

The letter I wrote to then President Reagan while I
was a patient at Roger C. Peace Rehab Hospital

2

The man that hit us was driving a pickup truck also. He had four other family members with him in his vehicle.

The accident occurred when the man traveling in the opposite highway crossed the median and came swerving and aiming directly at us no matter which way my father turned to avoid him. In a last effort to save our family my father hit the brakes. The man hit us head-on with an impact of 90 mph. He was traveling at 60 mph and we were travelling at 30 mph.

The impact was so great it brought the engine of our vehicle into the seat of the cab. My mother was left unconscious. My sister was left with a

-3-

broken neck which easily
could have killed her. I
awoke at the sound of the
brakes and by lifting my
head upward I was thrown
to the back of the cab,
then thrown into the cam-
per top leaving an imprint
of my body. I remember
hearing my father call-
ing to me when it was
over then I fell unconscious
My back was broken in
two places along with my
nose and my cheekbone.
My left eye was literally
hanging out.
    This accident would
not have happened if
the other driver had not
been drunk. (This was not
the first time he had been
caught drunk driving.)
The first hospital we
were taken to the doctor
was drunk! He tried to perform open surgery on my

-4-

mother's stomach out in the corridor, and also made an effort to sit my sister up with a broken neck. Meanwhile he left me in an isolated room for three hours before I recieved any attention. Thanks to the sheriff who was on the scene of the accident we were then taken to three more hospitals before being admitted to Palmyra Park Hospital in Albany, Georgia. There, later that morning, I recieved surgery on my back. By placing a Herrington Rod in my back to support the broken parts, the doctors saved my life. Six days later I recieved plastic surgery on my left eye, cheekbone, and my nose. My family and I were at this hospital for

-5-

three weeks and three days.
Now my family is
back home and I am at
Roger C. Peace rehabilitation
hospital in Greenville S.C.
Here I am recovering
from my back injury.
President Reagan, the
reason I wrote this letter
is because I believe there
should be stiffer penal-
ties toward drunk driving.
I also believe any drunk
driver that kills or even
injures an innocent person
should be confined to
prison for at least five
years.
As for the drunk doctor
I believe he should have
his license for practicing
medicine taken away.
I will hope that some action
will be taken against
drunkdrivers so that other

-6-

innocent people will not have to go through what I have endured!

It would really mean alot to me if you wrote back to let me know what you think about this incident and if any what actions shall be taken against drunk drivers. I still have some years to go President Reagan, but I sure have endured enough pain for a lifetime!

Sincerely,
Laurie Elmore

CC. Senator Strom Thurmond
CC. Representative Butler
Derrick

CHAPTER FIVE

The Return Home

WHEN I RETURNED HOME IN March of 1983, it was a major adjustment for my entire family. None of us were the same, and our family dynamics had changed. My parents had the challenge of providing for one disabled child while another was recovering from her serious injuries. This, of course, was coupled with the daily demands of work and trying to maintain a sense of normalcy in our lives.

It took years for Mom to recover completely from her injuries, though to the stranger she appeared fine physically. Kim was unable to return to school even though she tried. The discomfort and constant pain of the halo just could not be tolerated in a school classroom. Tutors came to the house to help her catch up with her schoolwork.

Being at home for the first time since Thanksgiving sparked new emotions and changes for me. Many activities that I had taken for granted were simply no longer possible. Kim and I were used to playing outdoors most of the time, particularly in the warmer months. We would run through the pastures on my parents' 150-acre farm, build pretend forts in the woods, and eat raw vegetables we picked from the garden. We would go down to the creeks and explore, looking for gold and diamonds. None of this was possible anymore.

I couldn't go out to the pasture and catch my Appaloosa, Pebbles, and throw myself onto her bare back, wild like a little Indian, barefoot and carefree. I missed being able to sit on her back while she grazed and kissing her warm, soft muzzle when she lifted her head toward me.

I no longer was able to run through the house with Kim or race her to the pool to see who could dive in first. No more climbing trees or chasing lightning bugs at dusk. We couldn't ride bikes or even take a simple walk. There was not a single aspect of my life that was the same.

Dressed for Sunday church

Before I left Roger C. Peace, I had been both excited and anxious about going home. I missed my family terribly. The thought of being able to sleep in my own bed again and continue my recuperation in the comfort of my own home was exhilarating. I understood that assimilating back into a normal life would be a challenge. However, I did not fully grasp *how* difficult until I was actually back home.

Navigating my wheelchair through the house proved to be a major challenge. The hospital had recommended that ramps be installed throughout the house and my bedroom and bathroom be altered to accommodate me. We lived in a ranch style home, but there were places throughout where the level of the floor changed three steps up or down, depending on where you were in the house. Installing ramps in every one of these spots was not feasible.

The wall between my bedroom and another small spare bedroom was moved, and a new bathroom was created. My bedroom wrapped around it, and I could enter the bathroom through a door that had been a closet previously. It gave me the independence of taking care of my own needs in a space that was big enough for me to do so comfortably. When I needed a shower, I transferred from my wheelchair into a rubberized wheelchair and showered.

Simple tasks that I did before the accident were a challenge now. Performing a task in the controlled environment of rehab was one thing. It was another to actually roll my wheelchair into the kitchen and try to retrieve something to drink or eat out of the refrigerator—much less heat up food in the elevated microwave. Getting a gallon of milk out while holding open the refrigerator door was tricky. The weight of the milk easily threw me off balance if I wasn't careful. If I tried to get a glass out of a cabinet to fill it with something to drink, my grabber and my situation did not always work together as easily as they had in rehab.

While rehab had been as realistic as the hospital could simulate it, the truth was that home life wasn't the same. Although my parents had remodeled my bedroom and bathroom, the kitchen was not completely handicap accessible. In addition to retrieving real items like glasses from cabinets and full gallons of milk and eggs from the refrigerator, I had to adjust to the physical setup of the kitchen being more suited for a person who could stand. I could not roll my chair under the sink to wash dishes or stand at the counter to cut up vegetables or even make a sandwich. So everything I learned while in rehab had to be "tweaked" to my actual life at home.

I was incredibly determined, however, to continue with some of the activities I had enjoyed before the accident. This included working in the kitchen. I loved to bake. My mom helped me by putting items I couldn't reach, such as bottles of oil, onto lower shelves. I could assemble everything I needed on the large tray that latched onto my wheelchair. It wasn't that difficult to mix together ingredients with this setup. No matter what I attempted, it never crossed my mind that I wouldn't be able to do it. It was a matter of finding a way to accomplish the task.

The adjustment was physically draining at times. Even with ramps, there were places I couldn't access easily. The tight spaces were challenging at times, but I eventually learned to adapt. If I couldn't get my wheelchair into a spot or up steps, I would crawl. One of those challenging places was our living room. When I went into the living room, I parked my chair at those three little steps and then transferred myself onto the floor and crawled. Then I climbed into one of the chairs and watched TV, played games, or read.

My family learned to adapt what they could to my situation. I refused to let my circumstances dictate my life or my attitude. Seeing other patients who had given up and had such a negative perspective scared me, quite frankly, during my stay at Roger C. Peace. Even though I was only fourteen, I could see how one's attitude clearly affected one's recovery. A positive attitude was so crucial for me at the time because I simply didn't know what my future held. Was God going to heal me? Would I spend the rest of my life in a wheelchair?

Although we couldn't play outdoor games like basketball, which we'd previously loved playing, we did have family games of ping-pong or pool. We also played cards and board games.

The kitchen/den was the most adaptable space to my situation and the easiest room for me to move around in. Because of this, I did a lot of activities there, including studying once I returned to school.

Like Kim, I did not physically return to school that

Kim and I with Grandaddy Matlack

school year. The school board also gave me the option of either being held back a year or having tutors so I could catch up with my original class. I was attached to my classmates and had done well in school up to that point, so I opted to work hard and catch up through tutoring. This worked well for Kim and me both.

My mother had already returned to work as a physical education teacher at the middle school, so my parents hired a wonderful lady to help take care of me during the day. She was so precious. She helped me with anything I needed. My schoolwork was sent from the school. I spent many days at the kitchen table poring over books while she cooked, cleaned, or kept me company when the tutors weren't there to oversee my work. Her presence was very comforting to me, and I came to cherish her. I really did not regard her as a babysitter but more like a friend.

In my wheelchair dressed up like a race car for a fall festival at Beaverdam Baptist Church.

My days were incredibly busy and most of the time left me exhausted. I spent a great deal of time on schoolwork. Not only the daily work the teachers sent home that my classmates were doing, but also the catch-up work I had missed during the four months I was in the hospital.

The support I received from the school and community during the spring was incredible. One day Mom surprised me with a trip to the middle school cafeteria where friends from my high school class were waiting to surprise me with a yearbook they had all signed. It was the first time I had been back in a school environment since the accident. I still treasure that yearbook and the moment it was given to me.

I would return to high school as a sophomore in the fall, but I had missed being with my classmates during the long hours I spent at home with tutors in the spring. I realized in a way I never had before the importance of school, the love of good friends and family, and where I fit into this special community of people. All of these seemingly little things I had taken for granted. That was something I would never do again.

In addition to schoolwork, I continued outpatient therapy. Once again, having a therapist like Diana, who pushed me toward accomplishment and shared in that accomplishment with me, was critical to my recovery. Although the therapy was hard work, I managed to recapture some of the skills I had before—some of them fun.

One of the things Diana taught me during outpatient therapy was how to swim again. Growing up in the water, I was such a water bug that the idea of being able to swim as I had before the accident was exciting. However, I wondered how I would stay afloat since I couldn't control my legs. I was determined, though. I really wanted to have the freedom of swimming again, if it were possible. Diana assured me it was. Once again, I found I had to trust her completely if this was going to happen.

For my first lesson, Diana got me into the pool near the rehab facility and had me hang onto the side. After I grew comfortable going around the edge, she gradually took me out into the water. Diana taught me to float again and reassured me that I wouldn't sink. Once I got over the fear of sinking, being in the water again was a great feeling—a new sense of freedom!

Before long, I was actually swimming. I used my arms to control my motion, and my legs floated behind me. It was exhilarating to swim around like everyone else. I played, swam laps, and turned flips underwater. The pool was the one place I felt normal. Soon I was swimming in our pool at home. Mom laid down towels for me around the edge of the pool so that I would not cut or scratch my legs inadvertently. Then I would get out of my wheelchair and shimmy down the steps one step at a time. Other times I went into the water at the diving board with some assistance.

Mom and Dad had a golf cart, so I had the freedom to get around on the farm as I had before. Again, it was a matter of being creative. I loved to fish, so I often spent hours down at our pond fishing and whiling away the summer months. Pebbles was my constant companion. She grazed in the pasture around the pond while I fished.

My doctors had warned me not to ride again, but Pebbles and I had different ideas. Horseback riding had been such a major part of my life before. That was what I wanted to do, so Mom and Dad agreed to help me. I remember the first time I got back up on my Appaloosa. Mom and Dad got on each side of Pebbles and, with a great deal of effort, I got up on her back with their help. Then, with each holding a rope, they stood on opposite sides of Pebbles and walked down the driveway with me on her back. It felt great to be up on her again. I gradually did more riding under my parents' supervision, but I eventually took over all aspects of Pebbles' care and rode her as I gained mobility and confidence.

When I was strong enough, I was able to take the golf cart out to the pasture and catch Pebbles with a rope and lead her back to the barn to saddle her. Mom helped me climb on Pebbles' back, and I climbed back off when I was finished riding. In time, I learned to balance on a bucket or fence and climb into the saddle. Although I couldn't take her to horse shows and participate due to the partial paralysis in my legs, I did retrain Pebbles to respond to voice commands. We became quite a team once again.

Unfortunately, the problems I had been warned about regarding horseback riding began to surface. I began to experience discomfort where the Harrington rods were placed. My doctor, Dr. deHoll, was also a friend who supervised my 4-H pony club. He explained how dangerous it was for me to be riding with the rods in my back. When I admitted to him that I had fallen off Pebbles, he warned me that if the hooks came off the top of my spine, they could possibly pop out of my back. I could suffer serious and potentially permanent damage. Because I was determined to ride Pebbles and I had healed physically from the original surgery, the decision was made to remove the Harrington rods.

The surgery turned out to be more extensive than originally anticipated. In my previous surgery in Albany, part of my hip-bone was used to fuse my spine to secure the rods. Dr. deHoll, my surgeon in South Carolina, had to chip away much of that bone to get the rods out. Once more, the recovery was a long process, but being able to take one more step toward the normal life and body I had before the accident was a great motivator to me in this recovery period.

During my recovery from this surgery, some officials at Furman University in Greenville found out about my accident and invited me to attend their basketball camp that summer. They waived the expense of the camp when they heard I was a huge basketball fan and had always attended their basketball games. I knew almost all the stats on every one of their players. Although I was in a wheelchair, they included me in as many activities as possible and found little tasks for me to do to contribute. I was sad that I couldn't be a real part of the activities, but it meant so much that they had reached out to me.

My three favorite pastimes—swimming, riding horses, and fishing—were an integral part of that first summer back home. To a large degree, I was able to use recreation to further my physical therapy and still have some semblance of a childhood. When I swam freely in the pool or galloped Pebbles across the field with the wind blowing through my hair, I felt normal again.

In addition to the physical adjustments we made, one of the biggest changes after the accident was our family dynamics. We all experienced a degree of grief over the lifestyle we had lost. Mom and Dad had a tough time with the daily demands of raising and caring for a disabled child. They did a remarkable job of rising to the occasion, but there were times when their limitations were stretched. Our faith in God carried us through those difficult days.

One of my own personal struggles was that my disability included my internal body functions. I had to learn what my body was capable of, how it functioned, and the signals it gave me. I had a catheter when I

Me with my catch of the day after a day of deep sea fishing with Mom and Grandaddy Matlack

first came home from rehab. Once I was well enough, I was able to manage without a catheter, but there were still times when accidents occurred because I couldn't get to the bathroom quickly enough. The humiliation was more than I could bear at times, and I had to guard against depression. I forced myself to focus on all the positive things I *could* do.

No matter what the challenge was, however, God always provided what our family needed. During this trying period, it was the blessing of a mother with a remarkably patient nature that encouraged me. Mom was an absolute saint, regardless of the challenge. Never did I sense a complaining spirit when having to clean me up, whether it was at home or in a department store.

On one occasion, Mom washed out my clothes and dried them with the hand dryer in a department store restroom after an accident. My mom taught me the meaning of Christ's love because she lived it. She didn't just talk it. No matter how humiliated I was, she was always there, reassuring me and reminding me to stay positive.

As I said, my relationship with Kim also changed. By summer, Kim's halo had been removed, and she had fully recovered. We still had lots of fun together, but it was different. We played cards—it seemed for hours on end—that summer. However, due to the difference of our ages and personalities, I gravitated more toward outdoor activities, while she enjoyed Barbies and other indoor activities. Much of this was due to the fact that I wanted to experience life out-

Me coming down the slopes on my special skiis and ski poles.

doors, being close to God. I had grown up really fast after the accident. My mind was not on imaginary activities anymore.

Some of the time I spent indoors, I wrote to pen pals around the world that I had obtained through church. It was also during this time that I met Henri, a French foreign exchange student who was staying with a family in our home church. We spent a great deal of time together at church functions, and it wasn't long before we fell in

My ski instructor and I in Crested Butte, CO

love. It was a wonderful summer, but he had to return to France in the fall, and I was returning to school. We continued to correspond through the mail until he returned the following summer. This relationship became very serious later.

When school started in the fall, the district office had special desks made for me. They were wide and hollow, like a table, so I could roll my wheelchair under and work alongside my classmates. I attended all my classes except PE, for which the county provided a physical therapist so that I could fulfill my PE requirement. Academically, I was right where I needed to be because of my home studies. Soon, I was rolling through the halls comfortably alongside everyone else.

By the middle of my sophomore year, enough function had returned to my legs that I learned to walk again using forearm crutches with AFOs on my legs. I was comfortable walking at home, but as a teenager, it was so much easier to retreat to the security and comfort of the wheelchair than to stand up and walk in front of my peers. It was another mental hurdle to overcome. I was sure everyone was staring at me and judging my appearance, most specifically my rear end. That proved to be a completely unfounded fear when I finally summoned the courage to walk through the halls for the first time at school. A teacher noticed me walk by her classroom, and she came into the hallway to congratulate me. Her class erupted in cheers and claps when they saw me. I realized then how silly I had been to worry about my appearance.

The struggles I had during this time came more from my insecurities as a teenager and the physical fight I was enduring to regain my health and independence. Through these trials, I felt a sense of God's presence fighting right alongside me. My friends and family provided support by encouraging me and helping me when I needed it. They also loved me unconditionally.

When my French class went to France the following summer, I was able to go along with them. There were many occasions when my classmates had to make a "seat" with their arms and carry me up and down levels of the French streets where wheelchairs or crutches weren't very practical. The trip was very meaningful for me because I was able to prove to myself that I was capable. My friends were so encouraging. It meant a great deal to me that they wanted me there. I had actually taken my wheelchair in case I needed it but never unpacked it.

In the years that followed in high school, my life was similar in many ways to my classmates. Henri and I were in love and unofficially became engaged (meaning without a ring). The relationship was really good for me at the time. It affirmed that I was a young woman, growing and changing, yet beautiful in a boy's eyes.

God opened my eyes over time, though, and I got to the crux of what was really important in a romantic relationship. When I finally found the courage to ask Henri about his faith, I discovered his view of God was very different from mine. I knew the relationship was over. For me, there was no question of whether or not God existed. God was so real to me. He had healed me. I didn't have any theological training at this point, but the Holy Spirit prompted me to have the conversation with Henri and revealed that Henri wasn't going to change his mind. At least, not then. I also believe there were many godly people praying for me during that time, which gave me the strength to break off the relationship with Henri. This was not an easy thing to do, but I had peace that it was the right thing to do.

God had other plans for me, and there would be another man in my future, one even more special because he would share my Christian faith. It was enough that God held my future in His hands. He was leading me down a path toward my future as an adult. This was a path that would be marked with excitement and yet also more heartbreak.

During the latter years of high school, God began to open doors and equip me for His ministry. I was invited to a small country church in Powdersville, outside of Greenville, South Carolina. Although I had sung many times for school and church functions,

Laurie Elmore

We are pleased to have Laurie Elmore return to our stage this year. Presently a senior at Clemson majoring in French and International Trade, Laurie has entertained area groups since her high school days at Palmetto. Her musical credits include placing in the 1987 Spring Water Talent Contest, a 1988 appearaance on the Spring Water Festival main stage, voice study at Furman, and appearances in many area churches. Come enjoy Laurie's music and message at this year's festival.

Newspaper advertisement for my performance at the annual local Spring Water Festival in my hometown

I had never done public speaking or given my testimony. The kids in the audience were my age. They believed, like I had, that nothing bad could ever happen to them. They thought they were invincible because they had not dealt with adversity yet. I didn't speak long that night, but what I said touched hearts. I could sense God using my story to bring glory to Himself, and it was therapeutic for me to talk about the accident. Sharing what I had been through encouraged and inspired others while also strengthening my resolve to be all that God intended me to be.

During my recovery, God taught me strength through adversity and ingrained in me the strong will to endure even the toughest of times. He showed me love and compassion during my moments of weakness and gifted me with the desire to reach out to others. I had learned so much about God and myself through the accident and my struggle to recover. I developed a real calmness when speaking.

I began to see how God could use me to touch others' lives if I allowed Him. Romans 8:28 (New Living Translation) says, "And we know that God causes everything to work together for the good of those who love God and are called according to his purpose for them." On many occasions, I sang in church and glorified God. I was still immature in my Christian walk, so I didn't feel the joy I should have when I sang. People shared with me that my singing touched them and made a difference, so I knew the Holy Spirit was working through me. However, it would be many years before I felt it too.

I continued to develop as a singer, and I participated in high school pageants, plays, and choral competitions. One of the plays I participated in was "Oklahoma." I made South Carolina All-State Chorus in my junior and senior years. Each school would select a few students to audition and represent their school; all of those selected would get to perform together in a concert. Overall, I thoroughly enjoyed the stage.

As president of the Christian Student Union, I led prayers and devotions over the intercom in the mornings for the student body. I was also a member of the student council my senior year.

Academically, I was a good student but more average than exceptional. My peers liked me and voted me Most Talented in my senior class. I was even recognized by the Optimist Club of Anderson for achievements made through my struggles during high school.

Me with my best friend, Meri, at high school graduation

Mom and Kim at my high school graduation

When I walked across the stage to graduate in June 1986, it was an accomplishment. I had overcome the effects of the accident that had almost taken my life and changed my family's lives in an instant on that cold Thanksgiving morning in 1982. God had plans for me, and in the immediate future, that included college. Whether or not I would attend college had never been a question, only *where*. My disability didn't change that. It made me even more determined to go into the world and live for Christ. I felt empowered and totally able to make a real difference.

CHAPTER SIX

The Prodigal

IN THE FALL OF 1986, I became a freshman at Furman University in Greenville. Doing so had been an arduous journey considering the fact that my SAT scores were low and my grades in high school had not been stellar. However, my parents were alumni of Furman, and that paved the way for my acceptance into the university.

I moved into the freshmen dorms, excited to begin my voice classes and make new friends. However, reality set in when I discovered, as many freshmen do, that there is a big difference between high school and college. Although I had been very popular in high school, I was a "nobody" at Furman. For the first time in a very long time, I was completely out of my element, surrounded by people who didn't know my history and who stared at me.

I had been the cream of the crop as far as talent was concerned in high school. If there was a solo to be sung, a lot of times it went to me. At Furman there were kids from all over the country who were much more gifted than I was. When I looked around at the other students on campus and in my classes, I realized I didn't have a clue as to what I was doing. I could sing, but I didn't know music theory well at all. My music education and preparation for the vocal performance degree were sorely lacking, which made it difficult for me to really click with my peers. This led to an overwhelming sense of inadequacy within me and added to my sense of not fitting in.

My intentions had been good after high school graduation with my plans to go out and live for Christ, but my spiritual immaturity and need for acceptance got in the way. I understood everything that God had done for me, but I faltered and gave in to those feelings, and I became more interested in the acceptance of my peers than in living a life pleasing to God. I tried attending FCA meetings, but I felt like I didn't have anything to contribute. As a freshman, I couldn't hold my own with the juniors and seniors. It's not that they weren't welcoming—again, it was my feelings of inadequacy that held me back.

The transition from high school to college was very emotional for all these reasons, and the attempt to adjust to my new life at Furman didn't go well. By mid-year I began to seek the acceptance of those who were popular at Furman, namely the football players and the students who partied on the weekends. I didn't drink that much, but I did want to be wherever the fun was. The approval that I craved from boys left me vulnerable to guys with less than honorable intentions.

I stopped going to church, not only because of my choices, but because I lived on campus and not under my parents' wings. There was no one to make me or encourage me to go to church, and the people I hung out with certainly didn't crawl out of bed on Sunday mornings to attend church. I had such a strong base in Williamston and at my home church, but on my own I didn't know how to get plugged in with another church.

I had always been outgoing within the realm of my high school and church social circle. I no longer had that safety net of church friends. Floundering, I reached out to the people who were most accepting of me. However, many times the Lord protected me during this period of "rebellion," preserving me for His ministry, although I was too naive to realize or appreciate it at the time.

One of the several people who tried to intervene was Adrian Despres, Jr., who is now a very successful inspirational speaker and Christian leader in South Carolina. At that time, he was part of the FCA at Furman and became concerned about the people with whom I was involved, particularly a football player named Randy. Adrian sat me down privately one day in a dorm room and shared his concerns. I thanked him, although in my mind I thought I knew what I was doing. I could handle anything, especially a popular boy who wanted to spend time with me and was willing to be seen with me. I was so totally in love with this guy (or so I thought) that I ignored my conscience nudging me to end the relationship as I had done with Henri. I also ignored the people who tried to intervene on my behalf.

At the end of my freshman year, I opted to stay at Furman to attend summer school and try to bring up my grades. I lived off campus with two sorority girls and continued down the path of the prodigal, a path which I had chosen. One week, my sister Kim came to Furman for summer basketball camp, but we didn't spend much time together.

During this week in June 1987, our home back in Anderson County was struck by lightning during a horrendous storm that blew through the Williamston area early one evening. Ironically, my parents had gone into Anderson to shop, which was completely out of the norm for them. The house was struck through a gutter, and the current traveled into the den and into the TV, causing it to explode and basically blowing that room off the end of the house. The main circuit box was in the adjoining room, and once it ignited, fire raced through the house, melting everything along the path of the electrical wiring. By the time neighbors saw the smoke plume and firemen arrived, the house was totally engulfed. It was a miracle that my parents had chosen that night to leave and that my father wasn't sitting in front of the TV as he usually did after dinner.

When my parents returned home, the police stopped them at the end of our road about a quarter mile from the house. My dad insisted that he needed to check to see if it was our home on fire and, after being allowed to travel down the road, discovered that it was indeed. The devastation that they must have felt see-

This was the end of the house literally blown apart by the electrical explosion when it was struck by lightning in June 1987

A picture of our home after it burned in June 1987.

ing our home totally engulfed in flames was unfathomable to my immature mind at the time.

As usual, I was off doing something I shouldn't have been while all this was taking place. I happened to be sitting in a movie theater with Randy, with whom I shouldn't have been in the first place, and to be listening as the storm blew through the area. To say I had guilt later about my home being struck by lightning while I sat there with Randy is an understatement. In time, I came to grasp that God doesn't work in that manner. He wasn't seeking revenge on me or waiting for me to mess up so He could throw down a lightning bolt. I felt guilty because I knew in my heart that this relationship was not pleasing to God.

My parents did manage to salvage some items after the fire was extinguished, with the assistance of the firemen who responded.

Old family photos, glass horses I collected, my mom's wedding ring, and other mementos were some of the things saved. A friend of mine who was a volunteer fireman sifted through the rubble and found several of my horses, one of which was a hand-blown glass horse from Italy. His thoughtfulness in the midst of this disaster meant a lot to me.

The neighbors pitched in to help my parents sort through what was left of our material possessions and spent countless hours laying out photos to dry in the sun and scrubbing items with bleach to remove the soot and ash. It shames me to say that it wasn't until I was older and had children and a home of my own that I was able to fully comprehend what my parents went through. I'm sure part of it was that I came home for only a short time before I returned to school in the fall and put it behind me. Looking back, it's difficult to say whether my insensitivity was immaturity or my brain's way of coping with another devastating event in my life. I had dealt with and overcome physical adversity. This was different—this event affected me materially.

My parents spent years rebuilding. The original house site was completely bulldozed, and they rebuilt on the same spot because of the close proximity to the pool. However, this time the house was constructed with me in mind so I would have easy access to everything.

In the fall of 1987, I returned to Furman as a sophomore, although I still lived in the freshmen dorms because of my disability. I got a single dorm room with a bathroom on the ground level. I had a golf cart on campus and could park right outside the door and charge it there.

During my sophomore year, I met Barbara Anderson, who was a music major but also a no-nonsense Christian who didn't care what people thought of her or whether or not she fit in. We got to be great friends. I was intrigued by her. She didn't wear a lot of makeup and wasn't really into clothing styles or jewelry. She was just Barbara. We started studying together, and she would sit at my desk and do her Bible study. Christianity was her life. She disapproved of my lifestyle but never took a holier-than-thou attitude. She was pretty persistent and ended up riding with me to a lot of the dances and parties in an attempt to keep me out of trouble.

By this point, I had broken off the relationship with Randy because of a DUI he had gotten. He'd crossed the one line I couldn't accept him crossing. Within days I regretted the decision and tried to work things out with him. He said no, fortunately. One night when Barbara and I were out, we saw Randy with another girl. I tend to get a little hysterical or dramatic when I get mad, so when I saw him with this girl, I went berserk. I ultimately slammed my fist into a cinder block wall, almost breaking my hand. Barbara was the one who calmed me down, asking, "Now what is that going to accomplish?" She was always there in the midst of my troubles but didn't let me off the hook. Barbara had a way of magnifying my foolishness and showing me a healthier perspective. God used her to "rein me back in" to reality.

She said, "You know, he's just a guy. I'm sorry, but he isn't worth it. You need to get over him."

I didn't want to hear that, so I didn't necessarily always respond to her in a positive, receptive manner. But God was using Barbara in my life at a very critical time because I needed to see somebody with a solid faith. I needed to be convicted of my sin, and that's what God did through her. He was calling out to me— one of His wayward sheep.

After that episode with Randy, I began to think about my life and what being a Christian meant. I knew that I had to decide whether or not I was going to live for Christ, but spiritually I remained on the fence into the summer. Barbara went home, and I went to summer school again and rented an apartment with another Furman student close to campus.

In addition to struggling with my commitment to Christ, I began to reassess other areas of my life. The doctors had told me when I finished therapy during high school that I could possibly manage with a cane and get rid of the forearm crutches. I started to put all of my energy into therapy, working out in the university

Hanging out in the pool with Barbara

gym two hours and walking three miles a day to accomplish this goal. Some of the guys in the gym were the ones I had partied with; others weren't. They weren't football players but guys who were serious about their health and their bodies.

Soon after, I was offered a part-time position to run the weight room, so most of my free time ended up being spent there. I became so strong that I could bench more than the strongest women—female swimmers–on campus. I weighed 95 pounds but could max out 150 pounds on the free weight bench press. I began to get a reputation for being a tough girl, serious about what I was doing, and the other people in the gym respected me for that. I finally had a peer group that liked me the way I was. They came to respect me, and we developed a mutual admiration for one another.

One evening when I returned the keys to the weight room after I'd locked up, a girl was sitting at the check-in counter in the gym reading her Bible. Her name was Sharon. We got to be friends that summer because I saw her every night. She always seemed to be reading her Bible, and she would ask me about spiritual things. It was so convicting to me for her to point blank ask me if I was a Christian. I had not totally cleaned up my life. There was no way to answer that question, so I avoided it.

It turned out that Sharon and her mom, who was a single parent, lived in the same apartment complex that I lived in that summer. She invited me to Bethel Baptist Church in Berea, SC, and I went to a youth meeting with her. Sharon was on fire for the Lord. Her passion for Christ drew me in. I enjoyed going to church with her.

I remember coming home one night under such conviction and thinking about the fact I had been "riding the fence." I was basically lukewarm in my faith, and that position was detestable to my Lord (Rev. 3:16). Even though it was difficult because of my disability, I got down on my knees beside my bed, and I said, "Lord, I'm either going to deny you, or I'm going to embrace you." I told Him how ashamed I was, that I had been acting like a hoodlum, drinking, and generally being a disgrace to Him after everything He had done. For me to have the audacity to act that way was shameful. I was broken over my sin.

God used Sharon and Barbara in a mighty way in my life, and I was incredibly thankful. He put them in my life for a reason—to protect me and bring me back to Him. I cleaned up my life after that—gave up the hard rock music, tore up my cassettes and threw them in a dumpster, stopped singing the rock songs, and stopped going to parties and drinking altogether. I also committed to God that I would guard my eyes as well as my ears and no longer see R-rated movies.

During the time I'd strayed from God, I had also given up my Christian singing, which was probably the saddest thing of all. I sang the required songs for my voice classes, which definitely did not bring me joy, but I'd lost interest in Christian music.

I had a lot of time to make up for—time that I had thrown away living in the world and not for Christ. I would make some radical changes in the next few months, but mostly I got reacquainted with God in a very real and intimate way, rediscovering my joy for singing. The void I'd been seeking to fill through relationships with guys was gone. I discovered a very real love—the kind that Jesus had for me. After I rededicated my life, I was sold out for Him. Many good things lay ahead for me now that I was back where I belonged.

CHAPTER SEVEN

Preparing for the Ministry

ONE OF THE FIRST THINGS I did after rededicating my life
to Christ in 1987 was to reassess my decisions since high school.
Enrolling at Furman University was one of them. I didn't feel
that was where God wanted me to be. I decided instead to apply
to Belmont College in Nashville, Tennessee. One of my favorite
singers had graduated from Belmont, so it made sense to me as
a music major–that's where I belonged. However, before I even
applied for admission to Belmont, I impulsively dropped out of
Furman. This turned out to be a poor decision.

Although I had reordered my priorities, my propensity for
making rash decisions had not changed. I had not suddenly become wiser or more mature overnight. I didn't even consider
the fact that if I wanted to enroll in Belmont that fall, I should
have applied in January. Since I hadn't, it would be the winter
semester before I could start taking classes. That is, if Belmont
accepted me.

Having made the decision to drop out of Furman, however,
I couldn't turn back. My parents weren't happy with my choice,

but it was a done deal. They encouraged me to enroll at a technical college rather than sit out a semester while I went through the admissions process at Belmont. So I enrolled in general transfer courses at Greenville Technical College for the fall semester in 1987.

During this transition period, I recognized again that my romantic relationships with guys while at Furman had not been healthy or Christ-honoring. My need to be accepted as any other girl on campus caused me to put these relationships ahead of everything else. I tried to prove that even with a disability I could get a guy's attention. That's one way I got distracted from my relationship with my Lord to begin with. It didn't matter that Randy or my other friends weren't Christians—and it *should* have.

But everything I had been through—the accident, the fire, and the relationship with Randy—jarred me, and God helped me to realize there were important things in life. Although I briefly dated a Christian guy during this transition period, I felt God's pull to stay focused on Him, so I was like a horse with blinders on—committed to Him only. I finally reached the point in my spiritual walk where I wasn't going to be sidetracked anymore. I wanted to be in love—with the Lord!

Most of my good friends were guys, however, and I did not necessarily want to end those friendships. Although not romantic relationships, they weren't necessarily Christ-honoring either, and the potential existed for things to go further. But I dealt with them in the same manner as my other decisions—cold turkey. At first, I distanced myself from these guys. Then I decided to become a nun. The plan seemed logical—until I realized I had to be Catholic. With time and prayer, I managed to put this part of my life in order and figure out how to live solely for God *without* changing my denomination.

The adversity God had allowed in my life had begun to mold me for His work. I wanted to be a singer and believed God had called me into that specific ministry. I was unsure how to make this happen because of my awkward fit into the vocal perfor- mance program at Furman. Believing the answer lay with Bel- mont, I went forward with the application process while attending Greenville Tech.

My first day at Greenville Tech, I arrived early to an English class and took a seat to wait for the teacher and other students. Two guys walked in and sat in front of me. I noticed they were body-builders because I had spent the last year in the gym myself, and I knew the type. They seemed like they'd be pretty cool to hang out with. They were chatting about a competition they'd been in the weekend before. One of them seemed to notice me, but since I was seated with my cane on the floor, he didn't no- tice my disability. His name was Kevin Thompson. He started talking to me and showed an interest, but I figured as soon as he saw the cane and discovered that I was disabled, that would be the end of it. I wouldn't have to worry about discouraging him. After all, I was *not* going to be sidetracked again.

My disability didn't even faze him. Kevin didn't ask me about the cane. In fact, he didn't seem to even notice it! He looked at me when he spoke, whereas a lot of guys I had dated before looked down or at my leg braces. Kevin was different, and he was definitely interested.

In addition to my commitment to God, there was an even bigger issue. Kevin wasn't a Christian. I carefully avoided situations where our relationship could turn romantic. We chatted casually during class each week, and he and his friend Kenny often talked about their weightlifting competitions.

One day, we were in the library at Greenville Tech working on a report for class. I sensed that Kevin was working up the courage to ask me out. I was standing at a card catalog when he came up behind me.

Kevin said, "You have the most beautiful eyes."

"Oh really?" I asked, thinking to myself, *Okay, THIS is going to be awkward!*

"Yeah, you really do."

Without turning around, I replied, "Tell me, Kevin, what color are my eyes?"

There was dead silence, and then he said weakly, "Blue?"

"No, try again."

"Brown?" His voice cracked.

"No."

"Green?"

"Yeah." I turned around and said, "The next time you want to compliment a girl on her eyes, you better at least know what color they are because it would be a lot more convincing."

I walked away, hoping that I'd discouraged him in a friendly way. By joking with him, I intended to send the message that we were "pals." As far as I was concerned, that's where the relationship started and where it ended. But I also wanted Kevin to see that I was not going to play games with him.

Kevin wasn't so easily discouraged. He followed me back to a table and sat down where I was working and asked me to lunch. I reiterated to him that we were just friends, and I didn't want to lead him on by encouraging him to think the relationship could go any further. We talked about my commitment as a Christian. Even if I were to date someone, it was not going to be a non-Christian.

Since I had forgotten to bring my lunch that day and had to eat out anyway, I finally agreed to go to lunch as friends. We drove separate cars to a nearby pizza joint and then spent the next couple of hours talking. I shared my personal testimony with Kevin and told him what God had done in my life. He seemed to accept and respect my decision. At any rate, he didn't press me to date him at that point.

By that time, I was a volunteer youth leader at Bethel Baptist Church in Berea, and I was very active in the youth group. With the issue of dating resolved, I believed God had brought Kevin into my life for a reason—he needed a personal relationship with Jesus Christ. I invited him to church. I invited many people to church, so inviting Kevin wasn't out of the ordinary. Initially, he politely declined and said he had other things he needed to do.

One evening, our youth group was going to see a contemporary Christian band, NewSong, in concert at Columbia International University (formerly Columbia Bible College) in Columbia. I asked Kevin to go with us, but he declined. In the following weeks, I continued to invite him to church, and he finally started attending. Before long, Kevin accepted Christ.

In the weeks that followed his decision, Kevin dove into the Scriptures and attended church regularly. He seemed hungry for spiritual knowledge and grew as a Christian. God really moved in his heart. I was ecstatic that God had used me to bring someone to Christ. For me, that's where my feelings stopped. I still had no intention of having a relationship and didn't realize Kevin still wanted one.

One day, as we sat talking in his truck in the parking lot at church, Kevin said, "I'm a Christian now, and I'd really like to date you. Would you be my girlfriend?"

Surprised by his admission, I had real conflict in my heart on whether or not to date him. I was so sold out to Jesus. It wasn't like after the accident when I was lying flat on my back and had nowhere to look but up. I had purposely chosen God and didn't want anything to jeopardize that. I would never allow someone like Randy back into my life, but Kevin had changed, and during the weeks of our friendship, I had too. My heart had softened toward him. If I was ever going to be with someone, it definitely was going to be a Christian and someone in ministry or at least supportive of my ministry.

I spoke with the youth pastor at Bethel Baptist about my quandary—I liked Kevin, but my dedication was to the Lord. The pastor encouraged me to do what I felt comfortable with because there was nothing wrong biblically with dating Kevin. I prayed about it and had peace about the decision. I genuinely believed we had God's blessing on the relationship, so I agreed to go out with him.

Meanwhile, I received notification of my interview and testing dates at Belmont. In order to get into their music school, I had to pass theory and vocal tests. Although I became more educated in music theory while at Furman, it was definitely not one of my strong points.

I had such a strong desire to go to Belmont, but wanting to remain inside God's will, I laid out my fleece. My prayer during this time was basically, "God, you know I'm stubborn, and I'm not going to stop until you slam a door in my face. If you don't want me to attend Belmont, you're going to have to make it very, *very* obvious."

That's exactly what God did. Kevin accompanied me to Belmont for the testing and a tour of the campus. With the pressure of the tests combined with my lack of theory, I flunked the testing to be accepted into the music college. I received a rejection letter shortly thereafter for the music school but was accepted into the business program. Having no intention of going to Belmont for their business school, I turned down the offer. Instead, I decided to enroll at Clemson University while I tried to figure out exactly what God wanted me to do. As for my initial goals, I felt I was back to ground zero. But then there was my new relationship with Kevin.

During the next several months, Kevin continued to grow in his faith, and our relationship deepened. It was gratifying to see him becoming a mature Christian. He was everything that I had ever wanted in a man and then some!

In December, after Kevin and I had dated for three months, we had our first serious discussion about the future of our relationship. I told him that I knew I could marry him, if he asked. He said that he wanted to marry me but wanted the timing to be right. He couldn't afford a ring, but I assured him that didn't matter to me.

In June of the following year, Kevin accompanied my family to Jupiter Island, Florida, for my grandparents' fiftieth wedding anniversary celebration. One evening while walking on the beach together under a full moon, Kevin dropped to one knee and proposed to me. It was so romantic.

I loved Kevin and wanted to marry him, but I had to be sure, especially about the issue of children. I was convinced, based on what the doctors had told me, that I wouldn't be able to have children. Kevin assured me that it didn't matter. He wanted to spend his life with me. His sincerity touched me. We were very much in love, and it meant a lot to me that he'd given marriage such serious thought. Regardless of my ability to have children or my disability in general, he wanted to spend the rest of his life with me, so I accepted his proposal, and we were officially engaged on my maternal grandparents' wedding anniversary.

We were too nervous to tell my parents about our engagement when we returned to the hotel, and it was late, but in the car the next day headed back to South Carolina, Kevin found his courage and blurted it out to my folks. It was a very long ride trapped in that big old Cadillac with everyone discussing our future. Dad was fine with the marriage, but he made it more than clear that I had to finish college first. If that meant a three-year engagement, so be it. Of course we agreed, not knowing how difficult it would be to be engaged for that long.

One of our biggest challenges was the physical side of the relationship. Three years is a long time to be in an intense, romantic relationship and not grow in that direction. But we were determined to remain pure before the Lord and for each other.

One of the things I discovered during this time was that pre-marital, biblical counseling in the area of physical relationships was sorely lacking for young people like us. There wasn't a youth pastor around who could tell us how to stay in God's will and have a physical relationship without taking it too far. No one could tell us the limit. The bottom line was "just don't have sex." So it was a trying time as young adults to balance our hormones and stay chaste when we were passionate about each other. We made the determination then that if the Lord ever blessed us with children, we would figure out how to counsel them in this area.

I started Clemson in the fall of 1989. In addition to being a business major, I also majored in French. I had fallen in love with France when I traveled there in high school, so it was an easy choice as a double major. It also would provide more diversity on my resumé. I continued singing in church and worked on that aspect of my ministry, but I finally accepted that I wouldn't graduate with a vocal or music degree. I took the talent the Lord blessed me with and used it to minister to people through church functions and other opportunities.

By 1990, Kevin was struggling at home with various situations and at the same time finding it hard to pay for college at Greenville Tech, where he was working on his automotive degree. After having a long heart-to-heart conversation with my father, Kevin decided to enlist in the military. This would provide him with stable housing and the money to finish college. Besides, the whole military thing really appealed to Kevin. So in February 1990, he enlisted in the South Carolina Army National Guard.

During the summer of that year, I went to France for an internship. It had been arranged that I would work as a bilingual

Me while in France during my internship, 1990.

sales assistant at Merrill Lynch in Paris. My lodging would be provided by a French family who knew one of my professors at Clemson. This family lived in an apartment building in the middle of the "City of Light." This was the lifestyle for most people who lived in Paris. Prominent families owned whole floors of a building and sometimes owned an entire building.

My host family had a whole building. I was accommodated with my own small room that included a sink, bed, and dresser. A community toilet was down the hall for everyone on that floor to share. We were right down the street from the French president's home, and I could take the bus back and forth to work like the French people did.

My indoctrination into the French culture was somewhat abrupt since I only knew textbook French, and my host family didn't speak much English. It forced me to begin speaking French fluently. I loved my job in the city, rich with its history and romance. From my office, I had a beautiful view of historical monuments, the L'Arc De Triomphe and Les Champs Elysées, to name a couple.

In addition to the apartment building in the city, my host family had a country chateau and a beach home in the North, which is where we spent most of our weekends. The food was incredible, and this family made me feel so welcome. I immersed myself in the French culture to maximize the whole experience and secure language retention.

After staying in Paris for about nine weeks, I went on to Versailles to join a group of other students from Clemson also doing internships in various countries. We took an international class at Versailles to officially receive credits for the summer abroad. It was a wonderful time of learning and experiencing the world.

My only regret during the summer was that Kevin and I were not together. Since e-mail did not exist then, we mailed letters daily and once a week sent tape-recorded messages to each other. The separation had given each of us time to grow individually, but for Kevin, he especially grew as a Christian.

Laurie Elmore of Williamston recently completed a summer internship with Merrill-Lynch in Paris, France. She worked with Mini-Tel, a service that gives clients Dow Jones information. Sh typed letters in French and English, followed movements of U.S. mutual funds and kept track of Dow Jones closing prices and the currency exchang rate for all countries of the world. Elmore, who suffered a broken back in a automobile accident seven years ago, trekked around Paris without difficulty during what she terms an "awesome" experience.

Article published in the Clemson University paper about my summer internship

When I returned home in August, I was pleasantly surprised to find Kevin even more on fire for Christ. He had matured so much spiritually. He was truly a different person from the one I'd left at the beginning of summer. God really worked in his heart during a time when Kevin was completely alone and dependent upon God. He'd left his family and me to join the military. He had only God to rely on, and his growth was remarkable. Upon my return, Kevin stepped up and became the spiritual leader in our relationship, whereas I had been up to that point simply because I had grown up in church and he had not. It was surprising but at the same time encouraging. I had hoped our relationship would grow in the way I felt God intended it to be.

Kevin enrolled in an associate's degree program at Greenville Technical College in the Automotive Department. He was gifted in that area and felt this would be a good occupation with which to provide for me.

My graduation from Clemson University.

Elmore, Thompson marry

Laurie Lee Elmore of Williamston and Ronald Kevin Thompson of Easley were united in marriage on Oct. 26 at the First Presbyterian Church in Greenville.

Dr. Randy Kowalski of Greenville performed the 3 p. m. ceremony.

Organist Alisa Carmichael of Greenville, harpist Joyce Fankauser of Spartanburg and the bride, as soloist, provided the wedding music.

Immediately following the ceremony a reception was held in the church fellowship hall.

The bride is the daughter of Mr. and Mrs. Wayne Babb Elmore of Williamston. She is the granddaughter of Mr. and Mrs. Carlos . Elmore of Laurens. She is employed by the Liberty Corporation Credit Union.

The groom is the son of Mr. and Mrs. Ronnie Thompson of Easley. He is enrolled at Greenville Technical College in the GM ASEP program.

Given in marriage by her father, the bride wore a white silk chiffon gown with French alencon lace bodice, wedding band collar, long sleeves and a full skirt ending in a chapel train.

Her fingertip veil of illusion fell from a fitted headband. She carried a bouquet of stephanotis and ivy.

Maid of honor was the bride's sister, Kimberly Ann Elmore of Williamston.

Mrs. Ronald Kevin Thompson   Nov. 6 1991

Bridesmaids were Barbara Anderson of Lexington, Ky., Karen Ellis of Atlanta, Ga. and Kimberly Fore of Anderson.

Attendants' wore tea length teal green silk chiffon with short sleeves. They carried smaller bouquets of stephanotis and ivy.

Niece of the groom, Courtney Dobson of Greenville, was flower girl. She wore a white dress with short sleeves.

Lindsay Dobson of Greenville,

the groom's uncle, served as best man.

Groomsmen were Kenny Wilson of Columbia, Norman Yates of Piedmont and Deni Vasilatos of Midland, Penna.

Ushers were the bride's uncles, John Travis Elmore of Greenville and Ty Matlack of Florida; and Jimmy Rogers of Williamston.

After a wedding trip to Edisto Island, the couple will reside in Greenville.

Our wedding announcement in the Greenville News

I finished my business and French degree the following year at Clemson. When I looked back over my college years, I was happy to be completing my degree but equally satisfied that I'd managed to put my life back on track. The transition from high school to college had been rocky, but I grew in spite of it. I'd made some bad choices, but God had been faithful to me. He sent Barbara and Sharon to draw me back to Him. I also knew, without a doubt, my mom and other women at church prayed for me daily when I was in college. God honored those prayers because, even though I was rebellious, He was faithful. Many times I had placed myself in jeopardy, but He kept me safe. He had again used adversity in a positive way in my life.

Now it was time to be an adult and get on with life—a life that would include a new husband and hopefully a ministry together. I graduated from Clemson with my B.A. in Language and International Trade in August of 1991. Kevin had only an internship to complete for his degree at Greenville Tech, so my parents agreed to let us marry. We married that October, turning the page from our college years and beginning our journey together as husband and wife.

My family with Kevin and I the day we were married.

Chapter Eight

Call to Ministry

After our marriage, Kevin and I didn't know exactly how the Lord would use us in His ministry. We were determined to live in the center of His will and be open to His plans for our lives. Meanwhile, Kevin completed his associate degree in automotive technology at Greenville Tech after doing an internship at a local dealership. With a business degree, I could have explored career opportunities in other cities, but I didn't want to be away from Kevin. Instead, I took an office job at a nearby credit union.

Almost immediately, I realized I had made a mistake. The job requirements were beyond my skills because I had not taken any accounting courses in college. My supervisor was a strong Christian woman. She patiently tried to teach me the business concepts I lacked in order to do my job. Within a couple of months it became apparent, given the scope of the job, that I couldn't perform what was expected. She offered me the opportunity to resign instead of being fired, and I graciously accepted.

Although I hadn't enjoyed the accounting aspect of my job, it had challenged me, and I couldn't allow it to defeat me. It had cost me my job. It was also a skill that would be good to have because of my business degree, so I enrolled in an evening accounting class at Greenville Tech the following spring in 1992 and successfully completed it with a B grade.

During this time, Dad suggested I work at Merrill Lynch, where he was a vice president. He believed I had the aptitude to be a stockbroker, and he really wanted me to be the one to follow in his footsteps. Since I was no closer to discerning what the Lord wanted me to do in ministry and I needed a job, I decided to give it a try. There was a certain appeal to following in Dad's footsteps and working alongside him.

Kevin graduated in May, and I began to study for the Series 7 test which I needed to pass to be a licensed broker. After I'd worked at Merrill Lynch for several months, however, I questioned whether or not I really wanted to be a broker. I had the background for it, having grown up listening to Dad talk about it. He felt with my personality and business background, I couldn't lose. I couldn't think of a reason not to do it except that it didn't make me particularly happy, but that didn't seem like a good enough reason to quit. After I had studied hard for a year, Dad sent me to Atlanta, Georgia, for a cram prep class over a long weekend prior to the test.

After that, I registered to take the test in Charlotte, North Carolina, but I had serious misgivings. Confused about my direction in life and feeling pressure from my father to continue in my job, I did what I had done in the past—I prayed. More specifically, I laid out a fleece as Gideon did in the Old Testament. I said, "Lord, I don't know if this is what you want me to do. If this is not where you want me, then don't let me pass this test."

I had to score at least a seventy on the test to get my license. I went into the exam determined to do my very best, but my final score was just shy by a few points of passing. With my perfectionist personality, I was devastated that my best had not been good enough. But I was willing to accept the outcome. I was not meant to be a stockbroker. I felt that I had God's answer.

Of course, my dad didn't see it that way. He thought I should retake the exam. In his mind, it was silly for me to take failure as a sign from God. In retrospect, I'm sure I could have passed the test on another try. However, I had laid out my fleece, and in my heart I really felt I had received my answer. If I had passed the test, I would have given the job my best but probably been miserable. God knew this, and I had to trust His guidance.

Kevin and I still believed I should be in ministry. I needed to take the next step, whatever that was, and not continue to flounder in office jobs. Although I sang in church, I knew God called me to do more. I sought out others for advice—my mom, my grandmother, church leaders, and close friends—and got the same counsel. It was obvious to everybody else, as well, that I should be in some sort of ministry. In order to do this, I felt I needed to get a ministry degree. Kevin supported that idea wholeheartedly.

I happened to run into a man at church one day whose daughter was an acquaintance of mine. He worked for Campus Crusade for Christ, and Kevin and I had helped him move a few months earlier. We got into a conversation about seminaries, and he suggested we drive down to Columbia International University in Columbia, South Carolina. It is a non-denominational school and offers many master's degrees in fields such as counseling and evangelism. We took his advice and scheduled a visit.

Kevin and I were very excited as we traveled to CIU. When we turned off the main highway in Columbia onto the long boulevard that runs down to the administrative building on campus, the strangest feeling came over me.

I turned to Kevin and said, "I've been here before. I've been to this campus!"

When I'd first heard about the college, I thought I didn't know about it. But when I thought back, I realized it was the location of the concert to which I had invited Kevin when we first met at Greenville Tech! The concert was at night so I couldn't see much, but I remembered that entrance specifically.

I sensed in my spirit as soon as we turned onto that boulevard that CIU was where I was supposed to be. Before I met with anybody in the administrative building, before I talked to anybody about what my major would be, I felt the presence of the Holy Spirit on campus the moment we arrived. I looked at Kevin and said, "I've been here before, and this is where God wants me now."

We talked to the college advisers about the master's programs CIU offered and toured the campus. Kevin and I left feeling very thankful that God had led us there. We drove back to Greenville that evening, satisfied that CIU was the seminary I should attend.

Kevin requested a transfer to Columbia through the National Guard where he worked full time as an automotive technician. He was granted the transfer, and I enrolled in the master of evangelism program at CIU. Though we would end up in married student housing on campus a year and a half later, our first home in Columbia was an apartment about ten minutes from campus. God really blessed us in making a path for everything to work out smoothly and conveniently.

Within the first year of our being in Columbia, Kevin decided that he wanted to go to Bible College too. Many of his co-workers routinely asked him questions about the Bible. He had to come home and ask where to find certain passages. We looked through the Scriptures together, and then one night he said, "I need to know this. You've been a Christian a lot longer than I have, and I don't know the Bible. I want to go to Bible College."

I was thrilled, but we were both concerned about how he would attend school and keep his full-time job with the National Guard. He applied for classes at CIU and discovered that the school was looking for a senior mechanic to take charge of a fleet of about thirty-five campus vehicles. Kevin was in a quandary about whether or not to leave a secure and good-paying job to take a position where forty percent of his income would be based on donations. He was just too nervous about doing that. Once again, the Lord was patient with our human nature, guiding us where He wanted us to be.

Kevin returned to CIU a few months later and found the position was still open. He worked out an arrangement where he could take classes and stay late in the evening on his job to make up the hours he missed for class. Kevin had a thirst for biblical knowledge, and he balanced working full time with being a full-time student and studying on his off time. He really wanted the degree.

During my second year at CIU, I worked full time for the assistant dean of the seminary. I also took counseling classes because I had switched my degree focus from evangelism to counseling, not really knowing what I'd do with the evangelism degree. I headed down the path I felt the Lord had laid out for me, though I didn't know where it was leading or how He was going to use me for His work.

I have such a heart for those who are suffering, and since I enjoy interacting with people, counseling seemed like a natural fit. I took several psychology classes during those two years because I really didn't have that background from Clemson. As part of the counseling degree, I had to do counseling internships. The deeper I dove into the program, however, the more I realized that while the coursework would be helpful in any ministry I undertook, I didn't have the personality to deal with other people's problems professionally at that point in my life. I don't respond well to "whining," and people who don't want to help themselves frustrate me.

When people came to me for counseling, I gave them Scriptures that addressed their situation, but they didn't seem particularly interested in applying them. It frustrated me to watch them listen and then walk away and choose their own course. Then they would have the audacity to come back and complain more! Frankly, it made me mad.

The turning point came one day when a girl came into the crisis pregnancy center where I volunteered. I shared Scripture with her, and she let me know she didn't believe it. When she walked out the door, I knew she was going to have an abortion. Something snapped inside me, I'm not even sure what, but I was not going to let her out of that room until she changed her mind. I think I scared her, but I wasn't going to do anything physical. I only wanted to talk some sense into her. I think I said something along the lines of,

"Your baby's blood is not going to be on my hands. You need to sit here until the truth gets through to you." My supervisor ended up having to intervene and let the girl leave.

Knowing that if I continued in the counseling degree, it would become my full-time job, frustrated me. I'm a compassionate person, and I can inspire people, but I had gone through a tragedy and had fought my way back, and I felt others should do the same. I didn't have the tolerance for other people's lack of commitment to change or, worse yet, an inability to be penetrated by the truth of God's Word. It was unclear as to whether or not it was a personal problem or perhaps not where God wanted me, but it was very clear He had not given me the gift for counseling at that particular moment in my life. I lacked the patience and ability to trust God when a client walked away.

After that experience, I came home and told Kevin that I couldn't continue in the program. If people were going to come to me for counseling and then walk away and not do what I told them, why were they coming? What difference was I making? I just couldn't do it. I became too personally involved with the people seeking help. I couldn't plant the seed, let them walk out of the door, make their mistakes, and live with it. At the time, I felt I had wasted two years of my life, except for the Bible certificate I ultimately received, but many years later the counseling classes played a key role in my later degree and then in securing a job within a women's ministry.

My academic adviser was not surprised by my decision. I was floored by his response. He said, "I see you in your own ministry, being a writer, an inspirational speaker, and a singer—impacting people in that way. That's going to be your ministry."

My initial reaction was silence. I'd never had anyone spell out to me in specifics what they felt the Lord was calling me to do. I said, "You've got to be kidding. Do you really think I'm going to do that?"

He said, "Yes."

His words seemed prophetic. About two years later, I published my first article and officially started my ministry, calling it Count It All Joy Ministries. Today it is known as Laurie Thompson Ministries.

During that time, I became pregnant. To say this was a surprise is an understatement. My doctors had always told me I wouldn't have children, but they had been wrong about everything else, so we decided to try. Kevin and I were overjoyed, but we had to make some adjustments in our lives to prepare for a child. One of the biggest was figuring out smart ways for me to get around with a baby.

Kevin and I when I was pregnant with Luke, our firstborn

Kevin built a ramp outside of the trailer so I could get a stroller in and out with ease. One day Kevin was painting the ramp and throwing sand on it to give it a rough surface for rainy days so I would not slip. God spoke to him and told him He wanted him in full-time ministry also.

At that point, everything shifted for us as a couple because I always knew I would work in a church or some other full-time ministry. This was new for Kevin. Instead of taking classes to learn the Bible better, he would have to get his bachelor's degree in Bible because he only had an associate's degree from Greenville Tech. It was the beginning of another journey for us because we were preparing for our baby at the same time. I started to consider that maybe God had used *me* to get Kevin right where He needed him.

I gave birth to our first child, a son we named Luke Elmore Thompson, in 1996. I became a full-time stay-at-home mom and supported Kevin emotionally while he finished his degree. He was still in the National Guard one weekend a month and worked full time with the school in addition to taking classes full time.

The transition from working full time to staying at home went smoother than I had imagined. I had been resistant initially because I had always been so independent. I never saw myself not working and had never planned to be a stay-at-home mom because I wasn't supposed to be able to even have children. We had to work through that as a couple because Kevin felt I should stay at home, and in my heart I knew that's what God wanted. God honored that decision.

I flourished in my role as a mom and had the support of other student families in the on-campus housing. Many of the mothers home schooled their children.

I wasn't as active as I had been because it was difficult for me to get out. We lived in a very hilly area, so pushing Luke in the stroller was a challenge. I didn't venture out very far on my own, but there were plenty of women around to help and encourage me as a new mother. This was a really good period of time in our lives.

Me with Joni Eareckson Tada at Columbia International University

We developed several strong friendships with other families training for full-time ministry. To this day, we have missionary friends serving in countries all over the world.

During the next two years, we were active in the First Baptist Church in Columbia. Kevin served as an associate deacon, and he taught Sunday school. I was a soloist for the choir. I didn't worry about finishing my master's degree. Most of the classes I had taken would transfer to another college if I had the opportunity to attend one in the future. I wasn't sure how the counseling classes would fit into that, or whether they would count toward a different degree, but I didn't worry about it.

Taking care of Luke seemed easy enough that I thought I could manage with two children. If we had another child, we wanted them to be two years apart, so Kevin and I started trying to conceive again. I got pregnant in December of 1997, and by January began having problems I'd not had in my first pregnancy. Starting at nine weeks into the pregnancy, I had excruciating pain from the baby lying in a position that put pressure on my sciatic nerve, which caused the pain to shoot down my right leg. I also felt sick all the time—at least through the second semester.

Kevin was set to graduate the following year. He began talking to people within the church and at CIU about what kind of work he might do. They advised him to continue with his education and get a master of divinity degree, which is what most people in ministry obtain. He was also advised to get the degree from a school <u>other</u> than CIU because the diversity of training would look better on his resume.

After researching several seminaries, we narrowed it down to a seminary in Texas, where we initially felt was the place for us. However, we decided the wise thing would be to drive to Texas and walk through the campus and meet with advisers as we had done with CIU six years before. Fortunately, this was during a stretch of time in early spring when I felt well enough to travel. We left Luke with Mom and Dad and drove to Texas. Almost immediately upon our arrival, we knew it was *not* the place for us. We didn't feel God's presence in the way we expected and didn't have a peace about relocating our family there.

We were mystified as to what to do next. We called back to South Carolina and talked to our pastor, who suggested we drive up to South-eastern Baptist Seminary in Wake Forest, North Carolina. His son attended the school and gave it a solid recommendation. He encouraged us

Me with Grandaddy Matlack

to see the campus, check into the programs offered, and explore the possibility that God might want us there. So we stopped at Mom and Dad's to see Luke and then drove up to Wake Forest.

The president of Southeastern at the time, Dr. Paige Patterson, happened to be in his office on campus that day. He agreed to meet with us, and he graciously answered our questions about the seminary. After meeting him, seeing how he led the school, meeting some faculty, and looking over the student housing, we were convinced this was where we were supposed to be. We had a peace that Southeastern was where Kevin should get his master of divinity degree. As Kevin and I walked over the campus before heading home, we felt God's presence just as I'd felt it at CIU years before.

We started the application process at Southeastern, but meanwhile, Kevin had his degree at CIU to finish. My pregnancy began to take its toll on me after our trip. My legs began to swell so much that my braces wouldn't fit anymore. I retained water all over my body, and early Braxton-Hicks contractions added to my pain. My first check at the doctor turned up nothing, but a week later, another doctor discovered that I had started to dilate and my water had partially broken. He put me on bed rest to stop my pre-term labor. I could only get up to go to the bathroom and take a shower once a week.

The next week I was dilated even more, so the doctor said to put a potty chair beside the bed, and Kevin would have to bathe me in bed. Even this did not help, so the doctor put me on medication to control the contractions and warned that if it didn't work, he'd admit me to the hospital. It was too dangerous for the baby if the labor continued. We needed another three weeks to put the baby in the safe zone of thirty-six weeks so the lungs would be developed enough to allow a safe delivery. We prayed diligently for those three weeks.

The women in student housing and at First Baptist were so helpful in taking care of me through all of this. Kevin had classes to finish and a job to go to, so these women set up a system of taking turns coming in to aid me when he wasn't home. My sister and Mom also drove down from Anderson periodically and helped when they could. I had all my needs provided for, and Luke was taken care of during this time. God really blessed me with a multitude of Christian women who put their faith into action by caring for me during my time of need and by providing all of our meals.

Unfortunately, none of the medications or bed rest stopped the contractions, so I was admitted to the hospital. After ten more days of holding off the birth, the day came for our baby to be born. It was a girl! Lydiaruth Logan Thompson was born on September 24. She was a beautiful, dainty little girl with red hair and a strong set of lungs.

Now I had two little ones at home to manage, but I'd settled into a good routine with Luke, and the arrival of Lydiaruth wasn't that much harder. Luke was a toddler and could get around on his own. I never tried to carry Luke as a baby and didn't want to try with Lydiaruth. Any time I moved around inside or outside of the trailer, I put the baby in the stroller and transported her that way. I didn't trust myself to carry her and risk falling. Using the stroller inside proved to be the best way of getting around without carrying my children.

The following May, in 1999, Kevin graduated, and I received my Bible certificate from CIU. In my heart I was at peace with the years spent at CIU. Although I had not accomplished what I'd set out to do, I learned and grew as a Christian. I became a mother, and my husband had been called into full-time ministry. I looked back on our time spent there as successful because I could clearly see God's hand.

Kevin resigned his position as the mechanic at CIU, and we moved to Wake Forest in North Carolina. We had an apartment in student housing at Southeastern, but Kevin didn't have a job. Talk about faith. We showed up trusting God to work things out—and *that* He did!

Within two weeks, Kevin got a job as a security officer in the Research Triangle Park of Raleigh. He worked in the evenings and attended school during the day. Later, he moved into a position with FedEx as a pickup driver, and he held that job for the remainder of our time there. The seminary told me about a master of divinity degree in women's studies, but with two small children, I didn't see any way I could enroll at that time. I tucked the information away in the back of my mind for future reference.

Not only was I busy with Luke and Lydiaruth, but my ministry had really begun to flourish. By this time, I had two magazine articles published. God opened doors for me with speaking and singing engagements locally and throughout the South and East Coast. During those first two years we were at Southeastern, I had many opportunities. Although I had not started writing songs yet, I recorded a CD of my favorite contemporary Christian songs, and I sold those CDs at my concerts. I also had an agent at this time, and he helped secure bookings for me.

During our time in seminary, we considered several different ministry options to pursue following graduation. Kevin did not feel led to be a full-time pastor, and though the Lord was opening doors for chaplaincy in some capacity, we also were looking at missions, both home and abroad. In the summer of 2000, we had the opportu-

nity to go on a mission trip to Moldova with our church in Wake Forest. At that time, Moldova was categorized as a third world country. Our team would lead vacation

Me with another ministry team member in the maximum security women's prison in Moldova

Bible schools for children in Chisinau, help with construction of a church, and visit maximum security prisons to share the gospel.

This trip was a life-changing experience for Kevin and me both, as our hearts were touched deeply by the spiritual and physical needs in Moldova. We witnessed, firsthand, children coming to Christ and desperate souls in the men's and women's prisons finding true freedom in the gospel. We could see what an impact we were having as the light of God's Word penetrated darkness and hopelessness.

At a women's maximum security prison that housed mainly convicted murderers, I was warned not to have physical contact with the female prisoners. Many had hepatitis, tuberculosis, or AIDS. As I sang and shared my testimony, these women fell at my feet weeping. Despite the warnings from the guards and translators, I gave these women what they needed—physical contact. I hugged them and shared Jesus' love with them. This experience had a deep impact on me spiritually. My sensitivity to the Holy Spirit was growing.

In the enthusiasm of the trip, I was not as cautious as I should

Me sitting on a little stool shoveling sand while helping with the construction of a church in Moldova

have been physically. One day as our group was helping to make concrete for the construction of a church, I was sitting on a hard wood stool and shoveling sand into buckets for the other workers. The twisting, turning, and heaving took a toll on my derriere. That evening, to my horror, I discovered a very large and gaping pressure sore on my bottom. I had brought antibiotics to prevent a urinary tract infection but no medical supplies for this type of injury. Due to the extent of the pressure sore, it became imperative that I receive medical attention at once. The pastor of our sister church in Chisinau knew a doctor who was a Christian and who worked at the small clinic downtown. He made an appointment for me to meet with her. Upon inspection of the wound, she told me it was very deep and dangerous but that if I kept it clean and applied topical antibacterial salve for the remainder of our time in Moldova, I should be fine until we made it back to the United States.

That incident was a real wake-up call for Kevin and me. We both realized that overseas missions might not be the best option for us due to my physical challenges and the medical care I required. Upon our return to the US, I recovered completely from the pressure sore with the assistance of oral antibiotics. Though we were both saddened that the door of full-time overseas ministry was closed, we looked with anticipation to see what window of ministry opportunity would be opened.

With the children a little older, I began to seriously consider the master of divinity degree in women's studies. As I checked into the degree further, I discovered that Southeastern would accept my counseling credits from CIU. Almost fifty-six hours would transfer over. When I added those in, I discovered that if I took one class each semester, I could finish the degree at about the same time Kevin finished his master of divinity degree. We could possibly walk together at graduation. So that became my goal.

Kevin had continued in the National Guard when we moved to North Carolina. His unit was stationed right across the border in Virginia. He'd drive up one weekend a month for drilling. He switched his vocation from being a mechanic to a chaplain assistant, which was basically a chaplain in training, and filled in as an interim chaplain for five units in Virginia. He would be promoted to chaplain once he completed officer training school and received his master of divinity degree.

In May of 2001, we took a family vacation to Nashville, Tennessee so I could compete in a talent showcase at the Opryland Hotel. A recording company sponsored the event, and the winner would receive a contract for a recording project. I didn't win, but I did attend several very helpful seminars, one being on the art of songwriting. God used this entire trip to encourage and motivate me to step out of my comfort zone and try writing my own music. I found out over the next few months how much I felt inside as the creativity and inspiration flowed. Songwriting began to come very naturally for me, and I could not believe I had not done this years before. This was a major change, in a positive way, for my ministry.

During the summer of 2001, Kevin enrolled in officer training school at Fort Bragg, NC, and I took classes in Advanced Biblical Greek, studying the book of Philippians. Luke and Lydiaruth were old enough to take places, and one of the most manageable was the pool at the recreation center in Wake Forest. We went each day and hung out. The children were very well behaved and stayed right with me. Even though Kevin was miles away, we were able to have a lot of fun together that summer. There was plenty of shade so I could watch them swim, and friends of ours from seminary were usually there and could help out when I needed it.

During this time I spent around the pool, I began to write songs for my second CD. The Holy Spirit moved, and the inspiration flowed out of me. I hadn't written songs before, but I was able to be still and quiet and write what was on my heart. It was a time of really connecting musically with God. I wrote nine of the twelve songs for the *He is Faithful* CD that summer.

Kevin graduated from officer training school and returned to Southeastern two weeks into the semester. The next week, on September 11, 2001, the terrorist attacks in New York City and Washington, D.C., took place. Many of the men who had graduated with Kevin were activated and sent to Afghanistan shortly thereafter as the War on Terror began. Kevin would not officially be a chaplain in the military until he graduated from Southeastern, so it was unlikely he would be activated before then.

We began planning for Kevin's eventual deployment and what it would mean for our family, but Kevin worried about me. I still had not fully recovered from my pregnancy with Lydiaruth. By this time, I could not stand for long periods of time because of the constant pain from my sciatic nerve. I had returned to a wheelchair at least part of the day to pace myself and give my legs some relief. The doctors gave me two choices to relieve my pain. I could either use a wheelchair or take pain control medication. Neither was a good option, but with two small children who required my constant attention, I chose the wheelchair.

For several months, I saw different specialists who performed a variety of tests on me to try to pinpoint the source of discomfort. Very painful nerve tests were conducted on my hips and legs, and other scans were done. I finally had an orthopedic doctor tell me that a simple shoe insert might eliminate the problem; my right leg was just a fraction shorter than my left, and it appeared to him that this discrepancy could be causing my pain. He put a simple wedge inside the heel of my shoe and told me to try it. I could have kissed that man! He had pinpointed my problem, and the pain was almost completely eliminated. I praised God for such a simple solution. I found out later that X-rays revealed a break in my right hip, which apparently happened at the time of the accident but went undetected and undiagnosed or treated due to my other injuries and paralysis issues. This break caused one leg to be shorter because it had pushed the bone up into the socket.

Over the next two years, we continued with our coursework at Southeastern. In the fall of 2003, I discovered I was pregnant. We had been mulling over the possibility of having a third child. My health had improved, and I was walking more again. We had always intended on having three once we realized I could have children. The doctor had advised us that waiting a longer period between pregnancies would be better after the difficulty I had carrying Lydiaruth so soon after having Luke. We were undecided about going through a pregnancy again when I became pregnant.

Shortly thereafter, I miscarried. I was devastated. I hadn't really understood the hormonal change that takes place with a miscarriage. Even though I wasn't showing and was in the very beginning stages of the pregnancy, I had lost a child. My emotions were very raw, and I didn't think I could ever put myself in a position to go through that again. Kevin and I agreed that perhaps God was telling us we needed to be content with the two children we had, and we were.

But in January, I got pregnant again. I was really scared about the possibility of losing another child, though I trusted that God was in control and had allowed me the privilege of carrying another child. I did everything I could to protect my health and the baby's health. Within a couple of months, I started to spot blood. The doctor advised me to stay off my feet completely, so that's what I did. I used the wheelchair a majority of the time, even at graduation in May of 2004. I stood up just long enough to cross the stage and get my diploma.

Kevin and I were very excited at graduation. The difficult years of getting through two different seminaries, almost twelve years total between CIU and Southeastern, all culminated in Kevin getting his master of divinity degree and my receiving a master of divinity in women's studies and Biblical languages. Both of our families attended the graduation. It was a big moment, and we loved having extended family celebrate it with us.

Kevin decided to resign his commission from the military because he felt he couldn't leave me behind with three small children if he were deployed. He also couldn't stay in and expect not to be deployed with all that was transpiring with the military. He had made vows to me and chose to put my health over his career. I told him I would

Kevin and I following graduation from Southeastern Baptist Theological Seminary in May 2004

support whatever his decision was, but I didn't push either way. I wanted him to do what he felt God would have him do. His resignation from the National Guard became effective May 2004.

We were in a quandary, however, as to where the Lord wanted us to go after graduation. Our plan before we got pregnant was to go on the road full time with an evangelistic ministry. We had seriously considered buying a camper and home schooling Luke and Lydiaruth. All of this changed when I became pregnant.

Kevin never felt he had been called to be a pastor of a church. He felt God called him to be a chaplain. We both believed that God wasn't ready for us to return to our comfort zone of Anderson, South Carolina. We needed to be out on our own, dependent upon Him and not our families, so that we could embark on our ministries together.

During the spring semester, Kevin learned about a ministry that provided chaplains to the business world. He applied with them and was offered a position. We moved to Greenville, North Carolina, where we bought our first home, a little brick ranch house conveniently located in the center of town near Eastern Carolina University.

I tried desperately to maintain my health and take care of my two little ones, who at this point were not so little anymore. They were actually a lot of help to me. Luke was in second grade, and Lydiaruth was in kindergarten. They both attended a Christian school in town. The Lord blessed us yet again with a great church family. There were no Southern Baptist churches there, so we became members of a conservative Baptist church. Before long, the idea of a church plant for a Southern Baptist church began to be floated around by friends of ours who had also graduated from Southeastern. We were torn between either staying where we were already plugged in or being a part of the church plant. However, the idea of the church plant ended up going in a different direction, so things worked out for us to stay put.

In November, our son Canaan Ronny Thompson was born after an uneventful labor and delivery. We named him in honor of our Hebrew professor because we got pregnant while "attempting" to study for Hebrew. We wanted an Old Testament reference which reminded us of God's faithfulness since He had been with us every step of the way. Canaan's middle name, Ronny, was in honor of Kevin's father.

Canaan's personality was very different from Luke and Lydiaruth. From the very beginning, he was a livewire–very active and strong willed. Fortunately, I had plenty of help within the church and from Kevin and our other children.

In spring of 2005, it became apparent that Kevin's job and salary were not what they had been represented to be. We were having issues with paying the bills, and Kevin was insistent that I not work outside the home. I had my hands full with the three kids. But it was obvious something had to change. We were really praying, "Lord, what do you want us to do?"

We investigated several other ministry opportunities. Kevin met some chaplains who had clinical pastoral education experience in a hospital setting, which is extremely helpful for a chaplain because of the amount of time spent in a hospital. They told him about a program that provided a residency and paid a stipend while attending classes. He could be a resident chaplain and get paid while training.

At the same time, Kevin's dad's health began to deteriorate, so Kevin decided to apply for residencies in South Carolina in addition to North Carolina. There were programs in Spartanburg, Greenville, and Anderson, South Carolina. We put the decision in the Lord's hands and applied everywhere that had an opening, trusting Him to lead us.

Nothing was available in Greenville, North Carolina, where we lived. That left the two big training centers in South Carolina and the smaller one in Anderson. We eliminated the one in Anderson because of the salary package since I was not going to work outside the home. Kevin got offers from both Spartanburg and Greenville and accepted the one in Greenville.

We went to Greenville to look for housing, and immediately my heart sank. I asked Kevin, "Can we go look in Anderson and see what's available there?" I did not like how big Greenville had become. I preferred a smaller town.

We found a nice home in Anderson within thirty minutes of both of our families and convenient to Kevin's new job.

During the next four years, the Lord worked in many ways in our lives. Kevin became a chaplain following his hospital residency, first for a hospice in Greenville and then for Hospice of the Upstate in Anderson. After being a stay-at-home mom for eleven years, I returned to work full time as an administrative assistant at Clemson University.

Following a concert in February 2008, I noticed something which seemed to be in my throat. Normally, if my allergies were bothering me, I would experience the urge to swallow more often than usual between songs. Yet during this concert I was not having allergy issues, but I was having those symptoms.

Over the next couple of weeks, I became more concerned as I felt the pressure in my throat become more pronounced. Following an appointment with my general doctor and a referral to an ENT, I ended up at an appointment with an endocrinologist—a doctor specializing in thyroid issues, among other things.

After an initial exam, I was told that I had a small mass located in my thyroid, and it was putting pressure on my vocal cords. A biopsy was necessary to determine whether or not it was malignant.

I was faced with the very real possibility of the "C" word, and many thoughts began to race through my mind. I had not even turned forty, and I had three young children. My ministry was going very strong.

My fears were rational and real as I considered the possibilities of what this growth could mean. I began to feel overwhelmed.

Everything came to a head one day on my commute to work. I cried out to God and wept bitterly—verbalizing the feelings with which I had been struggling. I had been meditating on passages of Scripture that reminded me of God's promises when we face adversity. At that moment, I wanted to claim those promises. I told the Lord that I trusted Him—no matter what the circumstances or outcome. I knew that He was in control, and I trusted Him. Those words brought so much peace to me as I faced the unknown—as I faced the very real possibility that my voice could be permanently affected by any treatment or surgery.

The biopsy was a terrible experience, but the results determined the mass was benign. Surgery was not recommended because my doctor felt medication could control the problem and my vocal cords could suffer permanent damage. Ultimately, after a year of taking medication, another specialist determined that my thyroid was producing normally, and the mass was not uncommon. This new doctor suggested having it drained as needed. To this day, I continue to trust God with my thyroid issue. I try to be more aware of any increase in discomfort, and so far my singing has not been impacted.

God reminded me once again through this ordeal that His grace is sufficient (2 Corinthians 12:9).

On a sadder note, Kevin's father passed away in April 2007. We feel that one of the reasons God brought us back to South Carolina was to have those years of reconnecting with his family and being close as a support system for his mother and sisters.

For the most part, my health has remained good. On rare occasions, I've had problems with my walking and still suffer with pain daily. At some point in the future, it is likely that I will have to have hip replacement surgery. But I am leaving that in God's hands. Otherwise, my health is as good as ever, for which I praise the Lord.

Today when I'm at speaking engagements or performing concerts locally through my ministry, I often encounter people who say, "Do you remember me? I went to school with you" or "your mom taught me in school." It's been good to be back home in familiar surroundings and see the people I grew up with.

For an additional couple of years I worked outside the home and was involved in women's ministry on a variety of levels before realizing that my family needed to be my priority once again.

I came full circle from the days at CIU when I felt frustrated by people and their problems. I understood then that people had the freedom to make their own choices, but I didn't like the outcome. Because of God's perfect timing, I now understand that for people to succeed in their lives, they have to be allowed to make mistakes along the way and learn from them. My responsibility and calling is to communicate God's love and truth to them and trust I am planting seeds.

I've used my talents as a singer, songwriter, inspirational speaker, and writer. I've practiced the lessons I learned in the counseling classes I didn't think I'd ever use. Although I am often amazed by the way God works in my life, I am glad I serve a God so big that nothing takes Him by surprise. He is in control. He can be glorified through any adversity or suffering we face in our lives. That is the basis of my ministry and my life in general. Hopefully, that's what shines through each time I step onto a stage to share my testimony. He is faithful.

CHAPTER NINE

Embracing Adversity

IN LAYMAN'S TERMS, I BELIEVE it is fair to surmise that adversity may be described as *any* event that occurs in life which is *unexpected*_or_*challenging* in one way or another. Adversity can involve natural disasters, tragic events such as a car accident or the loss of life, but it can also be something which simply is considered inconvenient, such as a job transfer or even an unplanned pregnancy. In other words, adversity comes in all shapes and sizes. Whether you are one of those people who says the "glass is half full" or one who considers the "glass half empty," you still have the opportunity to benefit from the adversity effect–seeing adversity from God's perspective.

What we do with adversity is entirely up to us. God teaches us in His Word that *"all things work together for good to those who love God, to those who are called according to His purpose"* (Romans 8:28). Are we going to take God at His Word? That passage does not say *some* things; it reads *"all* things." What exactly should that passage really mean to us? Simply put, hope and confidence are resources which God makes available to us in the midst of *all* circumstances. Hope in a sovereign God who is in control of everything that happens—the good, the bad, and the ugly, as it has been said. Confidence that we will bear no burden alone. Confidence that even suffering can produce something positive.

Yes, that's right, I said the "S" word. Adversity inevitably causes suffering to different extremes, which may include physical, emotional, and/or spiritual aspects. With that in mind, may we also consider how the Lord tells us in Proverbs 24:10, *If you faint in the day of adversity, your strength is small.* That does not seem like a real boost for the self-esteem, but it helps us to keep things in perspective. It helps me to realize I don't want to be known as a "fainter."

This was really brought home to me a few years ago with my thyroid issue. The mere thought of possibly losing my singing voice—the possibility that the growth in my thyroid might be malignant—shook me to the core. I was devastated at the prospect of not being able to sing again, and I talked to God about it—yes, out loud. I shared with Him my fears and how much I loved Him and how I wanted to serve Him with every ounce of my being for as long as He would allow. I poured over His Word for verses that would encourage and sustain me during that uncertain time. I did not want to be faint of heart in that time of adversity. I wanted to trust God, and so I just kept saying over and over to myself that He was in control and that my gifts and talents belonged to Him. If He saw fit to do something with them, I could still trust Him.

In the book of Job, we see by example a man who loves God, and yet Job is a man who experiences tremendous adversity. Job is praised by His Creator for his response, and he is blessed beyond measure for it. In Job, readers are challenged, "Shall we indeed accept good from God, and shall we not accept adversity" (Job 2:10)?

In my life alone, I have been affected by a natural disaster (lightning striking and destroying our home), the sins of others (being hit head on by a drunk driver, receiving improper treatment from an impaired doctor that led to permanent paralysis), and I have faced adversity due to my own poor judgment and sin. I have faced a plethora of challenges and felt those effects manifested in several ways. The Bible teaches that we live in a fallen world. Just because someone is a Christian and minding his/her own business does not mean that he/she will not be affected by certain events. We should also recognize that any church or pastor who only teaches/preaches prosperity is doing a disservice to his parishioners because the fact of the matter is that sin is all around us, and we will all be impacted by it in one way or another. It is imperative, therefore, that we be prepared for adversity because it is not a matter of *if* it will come into our lives, it is merely a matter of *when*. Being proactive and prepared can literally be half of the battle. Being proactive toward adversity will also determine whether one will be a victim or a victor to this opponent.

Personally, I experienced the importance of having a proactive attitude toward adversity at a fairly young age. I continue to experience adversity in my life. Each day remains a challenge for me physically. No, I don't complain, and I am very independent, but my family knows I must push myself every day. Due to my paralysis and the effects of the 1982 accident, I experience pain daily in some part of my body. To balance out this discomfort, I must make the mental decision to sit and stand alternately. Otherwise, my joints get stiff, and it is difficult for me to move. I have spots which are still paralyzed, and that makes me more susceptible to pressure sores on my fanny. So, I must make the conscious effort to sit on seats with cushions so that I don't wear down those thin layers of skin, which could lead to a deadly infection.

Because I am a partial paraplegic and cannot feel my feet, it is difficult to do simple tasks such as cutting my toenails. Several years ago, I almost had to be taken to the hospital while Kevin was away at a two-week camp with the National Guard because I accidentally clipped off the end of one of my smaller toes. Due to my balance and paralysis, I fall more easily than most people, so I constantly must observe the ground as I walk so that I may be aware of any slippery surfaces or small items that could make me fall. Because of my lack of normal bladder/bowel function, I must drink predominantly water because I have a strong tendency to get infections which can cause scar tissue. I think you get the point and can see that my perspective is affected by my circumstances. All of these things are examples of challenges…inconveniences, if you will.

So, I have actually learned to not only anticipate adversity, but to try

Kevin in his dress blues

my best to embrace it. How can I do that? I have realized through my experiences and even through those daily challenges that I can have hope and confidence in my Lord—the One I serve—the One I was created for—my *purpose* for living. In Psalm 119:67, we read, *It is good for me that I have been afflicted, that I may learn your statutes.* None of us enjoys pain, but there is a certain level of excitement when you see adversity staring you in the face. If I had to deal with adversity on my own strength, I would do a quick turn around and run. But I don't have to face adversity alone. Better yet, I serve a God who knows what adversity and suffering are all about. He cares about the big things *and* the little things. Scripture teaches that we serve a God who can sympathize with us (Hebrews 4:15).

How can we embrace adversity? We must begin by believing that God will use adversity for His glory somehow and some way. That is not my opinion; that is God's promise. Secondly, we must exercise confidence and hope in the King of kings and the Lord of lords because He will equip us for whatever lies ahead. In John 16:33, we see that *In the world you will have tribulation; but be of good cheer, I have overcome the world.* God also instructs us in the Old Testament to *Cast your burden on the Lord, and He shall sustain you* (1 Samuel 3:18). Why does God give us these suggestions for life? Because He *knows* we will have tribulation; He *knows* it is not always easy to put on a happy face; He *knows* we will try to carry our own burdens. We, however, have not been created for such a task. When we try, we will fail miserably. We are not designed to bear pain alone; we are designed to have a relationship with God. In that relationship, we will find strength and help in times of need (Psalm 18:1-6).

Most recently, I faced a new challenge. My husband, Kevin, who re-enlisted in the military almost four years ago, was deployed on a fifteen-month home security mission. He would be stateside, but he would be very far from home for the majority of that time period. I must say, when I first heard those words out of his mouth, I was *not* embracing it. I think my heart actually missed a beat or two. Over the next few days, however, as I processed the magnitude of what would be taking place, I knew that it would be difficult. I determined right then and there, however, to be positive and trust the Lord. Instead of working myself up into a tizzy about how in the world a little crippled girl could take care of three kids—a teenager, a pre-teen, and a toddler, mind you—I calmly reminded myself that if this was God's plan for our family, then He would give me the strength and creativity I needed to manage. I refused to feel sorry for myself because the reality is that I operate on the Lord's strength and *not* my own. Each day is a gift from Him, and each day presents its own challenges. Hence my favorite and life verse, *I can do all things through Christ who strengthens me* (Phil. 4:13). My strategy? To take one day at a time, trusting Him each step of the way—not looking backward and not looking forward.

When I was a child, my dad asked me, "How do you eat an elephant?" The mere enormity of that task overwhelmed my reason, and I did not know how to answer. Dad smiled real big after a few moments of my silence and said, "One bite at a time." That mindset is key.

Has it been difficult working full-time, having a disability, and being both parents to my three kids? Of course! There have actually been some days when I wish there were a big hole under my bed so that I could just crawl down in there for me to have some *me* time! And yet, my situation helped me significantly as I worked in women's ministries because most of the women I helped were single moms trying to balance motherhood, schooling, and work—entirely by themselves. That "adversity" has helped me to be a better mom because I am focusing on my children from a new perspective. It has helped me to be a better wife because it gave me a new and stronger resolve to protect my marriage and be even more proud of my man. Yes, this more recent adversity has reminded me, yet again, that God is not going to give me more than I can handle, and His hand has been orchestrating my circumstances from the very beginning.

What a tremendous ministry opportunity this has been for my husband to serve as the sole chaplain to almost two hundred troops in our United States military! I can already see so many blessings from this challenge.

Kevin and I celebrating our wedding anniversary

A real blow came a few months into Kevin's mission when my father was unexpectedly diagnosed with multiple myeloma—a blood cancer. I felt that my world had literally been rocked, and I wanted to be there for my parents, but without Kevin at home to help me with the kids, I was very limited in what I could do. I was devastated at the thought of losing my father and wanted to spend as much time with him as possible. During those first few days following the diagnosis, I cried. The kids were fearful, and I tried to comfort them. Not knowing God's plan for my father was overwhelming. Selfishly, I wanted to pray for healing, and yet as I spent time with the Lord, I relinquished that fear and began to pray for His will in the situation. That spiritual transition created the peace that I needed—the peace that surpasses human understanding (Philippians 4:7). I missed my husband greatly, but God became my Comforter, and He sustained me in that time of uncertainty. We eventually found out my father's cancer was very treatable, but that initial fear and feeling of hopelessness just seemed overwhelming with everything else in my mind and heart when I first heard the word "cancer."

I can rejoice in knowing that God relates to those feelings, He knows that we will experience them. That is why God gives us His Word as a guide—a manual for life, you may call it. We might stray. We may even become temporarily discombobulated, but He is steadfast in His love for us, and He will always be there for us. We must exercise trust in that spiritual reality—*that* defines genuine Christian faith!

Daily, private struggles in life are important to the Lord as well. While Kevin was gone, some days were just plain awful for me. Some days, I just looked up toward heaven and would ask, "Why, why is this happening to me?" One such day that is embedded in my memory is a Sunday morning when I was completely ready for church. My hair was done, my outfit was on, and I had even prompted the kids to get into the car so that we would not be late for Sunday school. I really needed to go to the bathroom but decided to try to "hold it" until I brushed my teeth and put on my lipstick. That was a mistake. For whatever reason, I was not able to "hold it," and I did not make it to the toilet. It was an ungodly mess, and it was all over me, all over the toilet, all over the floor, all over my leg braces, and even on my shoes. Honestly, I did not even know where to begin in the cleanup process. Kevin is always so wonderful when this happens, and he cleans me up along with any mess on the floor, etc. Yet, I didn't have him there. I wanted to protect the kids and not embarrass them by letting them see me like that, so I managed to close and lock the bathroom door while still being in a state of shock. As the aroma filled the bathroom and I was desperately trying to figure out what to do first, I began to cry. "Why, God? Why did you allow this to happen? What are you trying to teach me through this? I am humiliated and ashamed, and I don't understand why you let this happen!" Of all the things that happen to me because of my disability, incontinence issues affect me the most deeply. I feel so helpless, embarrassed, and utterly humiliated by these occurrences.

An hour later, I had painstakingly gotten everything removed and had showered—again. I put the soiled items in the washer, spot-cleaned the carpet, and cleaned the toilet. As I headed out of the bathroom, I whispered a prayer. "God, thank you for letting that happen here. I would have died if that had happened at church. Thank you for looking out for me. Thank you too for using this experience to humble me." I was so exhausted, and I could not even tell anyone but Kevin what I had just been through. I texted him, and he was so broken that he was not here to help me. I reassured him that God had helped me get through it and that I was going to be okay. It was an awful experience and one that I am not proud of in the least, but I made it through. I trusted God in each step of that awful cleanup process, and He was faithful.

I now see adversity in a different light because storms *are* going to come—whether it is something due to my disability or something that deals with my children, family, job, etc. I know things are going to happen, and I know that I may not always like them. I may ask God, "Why?" and that's ok! I know that sometimes I will cry out in anguish because I do not understand—that is part of our human nature, but may I *never* question God's goodness or His sovereignty over all things. May I *never* allow my emotions to justify or excuse personal sin or worse, a lack of faith. May I *never* allow bitterness or anger to creep into my heart so that it becomes a barrier between me and my God. My prayer is that I aim for maintaining the mindset that whatever happens, I can handle it–with God by my side.

There are things in life that we deal with that will have "adverse effects" upon us. The "adversity effect," however, is a different perspective of that same idea–a play on words, perhaps. The bottom line is that adversity is very real, and it will affect each one of us—that's just life by and large. But with God's grace and strength, we will survive and be better people for it. Our sole purpose on earth is to glorify God (Isaiah 43:7), and what better testimony can we share with the world than how God has used difficult circumstances in our lives to demonstrate His sovereignty and love for us!

As you have read about my journey, you can see that God's hand was in the midst of everything that transpired. He had a purpose for me, and whether I ran *from* Him or *to* Him, He orchestrated His will in my life. There are basic principles that we can adhere to in life, and the most basic is that God's Word, the Bible, is TRUTH, and we can cling to what it says. We may not always understand *why* things happen in life, but we can trust that God is never caught off guard. Jesus once spoke to His disciples when they asked why a man was disabled, and He said, *'It was not because of his sins or his parents' sins,' Jesus answered. 'This happened so the power of God could be seen in him'* (John 9:3).

My story is but one of many. My prayer is simply that God will use it to encourage and inspire others in this journey called life. Put on your seatbelt, though, because it's a trip! I embrace the adventure with God as my Pilot, won't you? It may not always be pretty or comfortable, but the Creator and Sustainer of the universe promises to give us all that we need—we just have to believe it and embrace Him for who He is. Whatever we face, we don't face it alone; God will be glo-rified through it, and we will be stronger people because of it. And *that*, my friends, is the adversity ef-fect. And *that* is a concept which the world just doesn't understand—how something bad can produce some-thing good.

Me at the time of book publication

For more information about
LAURIE ELMORE THOMPSON
&
LAURIE'S STORY:
DISCOVERING JOY IN ADVERSITY
please visit:

www.lauriethompsonministries.com
lauriethompsonministries@gmail.com

For more information about
AMBASSADOR INTERNATIONAL
please visit:

www.ambassador-international.com
@AmbassadorIntl
www.facebook.com/AmbassadorIntl